Democracy Is Not Enough

Democracy Is Not Enough

A PERSONAL SURVEY

OF THE HUNGRY WORLD

BY JOHN SCOTT

Harcourt, Brace and Company

New York

B.3.60

Library of Congress Catalog Card Number: 60-5434
Printed in the United States of America

To my wife Masha,
understanding companion in most of my travels

A WORD OF THANKS

A reporter writes and talks—but mostly he listens. So in my travels about the world I have listened to many, high and low—the man in power and the man in the street. And I have been especially fortunate in being able to consult ("pick the brains of" might be more to the point) my friends and colleagues of *Time* the world over. I cannot saddle them with any responsibilities whatever for the thoughts expressed in this work. I would simply salute them, for they are a very special, a very knowing breed. The book, good or bad, is all mine.

I want also to thank Julia Fay Treloar, Marvine Howe, and Constance Dibble for their help in preparing the manuscript.

John Scott

Ridgefield, Connecticut
October, 1959

Foreword

This is a book about the underdeveloped nations and territories of Asia, Africa, and Latin America. It is a book about the nearly two billion human beings, most of them with yellow, black, or brown skins, who have not achieved the 50-per-cent adult literacy and the $200 a year per capita income mark which with some variation can be taken as the dividing line between underdevelopment and development, between the Hungry World and the sated world. It is a book about problems and choices, theirs and ours.

This Hungry World is of great and growing importance to the United States. It includes most of our planet's population and resources. Its restive millions, fired with new desires and hopes and armed with new weapons, are demanding and winning freedom—the right to govern or misgovern themselves.

As these new nations emerge through self-government to independence, they are looking for help and guidance. They are groping for patterns of thought, for a political and economic philosophy, for administrative and technical aid, for capital, and most of all for understanding. Until recently the only place for them to turn was to the West, with its Christian ideals of love and charity, its wealth, and its proclaimed political democracy. Today the Communist world presents an alternative.

7

During the past five years it has been my good fortune to visit more than sixty of these nations. As I traveled and tried to wrestle my observations into some order and meaning, my convictions grew that in the Hungry World democracy is not enough. That system of multi-party, parliamentary, representative government we so cherish in Western Europe and North America is not immediately adaptable to underdeveloped nations and peoples. As a political system it works badly in the Hungry World. And the Western powers seem unable or unwilling to meet their younger brothers' demands for capital.

Yet if democracy is not enough, what is?

I saw enough during nearly ten years in the Soviet Union to be convinced that communism's glowing promises can be realized only at the price of those freedoms the Hungry World so covets, as those nations which have fallen victim to Soviet colonialism could testify if they were allowed to speak. Yet it has been increasingly clear, particularly in Asia, that other underdeveloped nations are being tempted to try communism.

How can they be dissuaded? What better tailored framework of ideas and actions can an awakened West offer the Hungry World?

This book attempts to answer these questions.

CONTENTS

Democracy Is Not Enough

One ⦿ *Four Magic Words*

During my odyssey through the Hungry World, I found four magic but misleading words in constant and controversial use: colonialism, nationalism, communism, and socialism. What do these words mean?

Colonialism

As an American I was predisposed to be critical of colonialism. But before I had gone far through the Hungry World, I was forced to conclude that the colonial powers had done much to develop and benefit the populations they controlled.

Colonialism must be weighed in context. To use an analogy, in a cannibalistic society slavery is progressive and enlightened, for it is less unpleasant to be enslaved than to be eaten. By the same token, in a slave-holding society, colonialism is a major step forward, for in every case it has introduced measures of public health and education and has created the climate under which economic development can begin.

I was never so conscious of this as when visiting Ethiopia, that ancient mountain kingdom, independent since the days of King Solomon. For Ethiopia remains today one of the world's most backward countries, and many of the schools and bridges,

13

much of the meager industrial development the country boasts is the work of the conquering Italians during their short occupation.

Colonialism ruthlessly suppressed resistance, forced the natives to work for low wages, denied them freedom of movement, expression, and equality of opportunity. For all these reasons Africans and Asians are often loath to admit the achievements of colonialism.

These are, nevertheless, real. For however rapacious the colonialists' motives and however rich the stockholders in Europe may have become, economic development did result. Doctors, missionaries, engineers, teachers also came and generally with the highest motives. Many of these men and women spent decades of selfless service working for the good of the native populations.

To summarize the harvest of colonialism:

"Pacification" suppressed local tribal warfare, and some kind of order and security was established and maintained.

Cannibalism, slavery, ritual murder, and other atavistic practices were outlawed.

Elementary communications were created—roads, bridges, railroads, telephones, air lines. Though these facilities were usually established for the convenience of the colonists themselves, they were inevitably used by the natives. They opened up the country.

Public-health measures were taken against such scourges as the tsetse fly (carrier of sleeping sickness to humans and nagana to cattle), the malarial mosquito, and trachoma. In many cases these campaigns virtually stamped out diseases which for centuries had constituted the local populations' principal killers. At the same time, hospitals and clinics furnished improved therapy for everything from hunting accidents to childbirth. These facilities were inadequate and frequently were set up for the protection of the European minorities, but their effect on the native population was immense. In many cases life expectancy was doubled in a few years. In some instances population increases embarrassingly outran food resources—an unexpected and unintended result of colonial public-health activity.

Substantial progress was made against such chronic disasters as floods, droughts, locust invasions, and the famines which historically followed such catastrophes. Again, this progress frequently led to rapid population increase and consequent chronic undernourishment.

Educational facilities were created, though they were often shamefully inadequate and discriminatory. It is disgraceful that in Algeria, for example, in 1954, after 125 years of French rule, only one Moslem boy in five, one girl in sixteen, was in school. But it was an eye opener to see that in Liberia, independent since its founding in the early nineteenth century, the school situation is far worse than in Algeria. In Ethiopia until the Italian invasion in 1934 there was no public-school system at all.

In most cases colonial authority established some rule of law—the white man's law, to be sure, and discriminatingly administered at that. But it is interesting to note that as Asian and African countries achieved independence, they usually retained European legal codes.

Colonialism created conditions under which capital formation began. To produce enough food to supply the growing population, the needed machinery was set up—power plants, fertilizer industries, port facilities, soil conservation, and reforestation projects, as well as numerous and diverse manufacturing industries. Again the motive was usually profit for the imperialists or settlers, but the enterprises stayed even when the profits were repatriated.

THE COLONIAL POWERS COMPETE

Different policies and methods of administration were used by the colonial powers. Often these policies were influenced by climatic conditions, a temperate climate encouraging a "settler" colonization and stricter control of the natives as opposed to a "nonsettler" or simple administrative colonial rule.

The Turks and Germans were squeezed from Africa and the Middle East many years ago as a result of considerations having nothing to do with their colonial administrations. Both left deep marks on their former colonies; both were harsh but fair; both were relatively efficient.

The Dutch were pushed early from America and Africa by their British rivals but retained the fabulous Indies, which they systematically milked for more than three centuries, keeping power in Dutch hands at all levels and barring most Indonesians from advanced education or administrative experience, so that, when *merdeka* (freedom) came, Indonesia was probably the worst-prepared country of its size ever to become independent.

The early Portuguese colonists, rapacious and corrupt, were pushed from their immense empire by the Dutch and British in Asia and by rebellious patriots in Latin America. Portugal retains two large African colonies and several tiny enclaves and islands in Asia and Africa, where they remain today, nepotistic and backward. On the other hand, they do not practice racial segregation.

The Spanish, like their more tenacious Iberian cousins, were exploiters rather than investors. They were systematically pushed from position after position by imperial competitors and independence movements, until at this writing Spain has virtually no colonies at all.

The Belgians came late into the field of colonial administration and did well. The Congo was one of the richest and best-administered colonies in history. With a total investment of less than half a billion dollars, the Belgians gave the Congo an efficient, unsentimental administration and planned, steady economic progress and growth. Furthermore, the Belgians worked hard and saw to it that the twelve million Congolese shared the benefits of development. They barred small-time Belgian freebooters and insisted on heavy reinvestment rates and handsome programs of railroad, canal, road, port, and urban construction. But until recently the Belgians built few schools, and they deprived both Congolese and resident Belgians of the franchise or any freedom of political organization. The Belgian administrators prided themselves on the fact that, although their Africans had no vote, they had shirts and shoes—and many opportunities. The Belgians shunned the racial amalgamation tacitly accepted by the Iberians (on whom it had earlier been practiced by the conquering Arabs), but did not set up a color bar as such. In theory, they gave social equality to "evolved" Africans, but in practice this equality applied to very few—and strict racial segregation is evident in the Congo's restricted residential districts, schools, hotels, and restaurants.

Recently the Belgians have had trouble in the Congo. If they give way gracefully now and allow self-government in two to five years, let us say, and promise independence within a decade, they may avoid a major bloody rebellion.

British colonial policies have been more varied and complex than their competitors'. For at least a generation London has promised ultimate independence to all dependent areas except perhaps for specific strategic strong points like Gibraltar, Zanzibar, Gambia, and Malta. Anxious to atone for her rapacious behavior in some parts of the world during the eighteenth century, Britain has recently studiously avoided exaggerated exploitation of her dependencies.

Britain has worked toward preparing her colonies for independence and, as Indians, Burmese, Ghanians, and many others can testify, has in due course withdrawn, leaving the newly independent nation free to determine whether or not it wanted to remain in the Commonwealth. In most cases the advantages of sterling-bloc services and Commonwealth preferences have been such that the cast-loose colonies have decided to become voluntary members of that impressive association of free nations.

France's policies have been the most contradictory. In principle, France has been dedicated to the assimilation of her

colonies, to making Frenchmen of her Africans. But outnum-
bered as they have been until recent years by their colonial
citizens, the French have been unwilling to implement their
own principle for fear that France herself would be assimilated
by her own empire—a process whose results in ancient Rome
were unfortunate. (One French journalist recently wrote: "The
question today is not whether the French can keep Africa, but
whether they can keep France.")

Badly frightened by Algeria, the French have recently been
spending large sums of money on development—in the neighborhood of $200 million annually for all their overseas posses-
sions. FIDES (*Fonds d'Investissement pour le Développement
Economique et Social*), France's Point Four, and a whole series
of extraordinary financial measures have provided, in effect, for
the maintenance by the French taxpayer of much of the administrative expense of running France *d'Outre-Mer* and have built
magnificent cities, roads, airports, ports, dams, and schools from
Brazzaville to Dakar to Bizerte. These expenditures, most of
them on projects that are not even expected to render any
immediate financial return, are unmatched by any other colonial
power.

If they agree to recognize Algerian independence and if they
keep on spending money, the French have a good chance of
seeing their empire change within the next decade into a free
and friendly association of states, co-operating in development
and sharing in profits.

But colonialism is finished. It has become the devil-image of
the Hungry World. Within a decade, except perhaps for certain
small strategic strongholds, no colonies will remain on our side
of the proverbial curtain.

That the wave of postwar nationalist movements is destroying colonialism before it has outlived its usefulness in some
areas is not hard to prove. Again and again I found myself
asking Asians and Africans in soon-to-be nations: "Are you
really ready for independence?"

I got two answers worth recording. One was an analogy with the institution of marriage. "If you wait to marry," I was told, "until you are *really* ready—emotionally, educationally, financially—the girl has married someone else. You have to take it before you are ready. And so it is with independence."

Other Africans and Asians, full of newly gained knowledge, asked: "Was the United States *really* ready for independence in 1776?" Reflecting on some of the things which occurred between then and, let us say, 1865, I had to agree that we were not. But we became independent in 1776, and we made the best we could of it. And the Asians and Africans today are determined to do likewise.

To summarize: Colonialism spawned its destroyer—nationalism.

Nationalism

Nationalism is love, allegiance, pride, faith, hope felt toward a national entity.

Until recently most Africans and Asians felt these emotions for the family, the village, the tribe. Modern communications and education have awakened in the hearts and minds of millions the consciousness of their nationality. People who once knew themselves only as Shans or Kurds, Cantonese or Karens, have come to feel themselves Laos, Iraqis, Chinese, and Burmese.

Other millions in these new nations are still not conscious of their nationalities. I talked with people in Calcutta who felt themselves more Bengali than Indian. And in Sumatra millions felt themselves more closely associated with their island than with the Indonesian Republic. The governments of many of these new states are currently striving to arouse the allegiance of their citizens by whipping nationalism into a frenzy, and they are making it into the powerful political moving force that it has become all over the world.

By its nature nationalism demands independence from outside influence and authority. Like the calculus, nationalism can
be put to constructive or destructive uses. It can engender in a
people discipline and diligence or arrogance and aggression. It
can also be used or misused by outside forces like communism.

Communism

Communism is the dictatorship of a disciplined minority bent
on seizing and keeping power and incorporating it into the huge
world-power complex centered today in Moscow and perhaps
tomorrow in Peking. Theoretically, communism is based on the
teachings of Marx, Engels, and Lenin. Actually, most communists are simple servants in a power apparatus, though they pay
lip service to a Marxist-Leninist ritual litany, repeated, taken
for granted, but no longer analyzed, criticized, or understood.

To gain and keep power, communists sometimes use military
force; sometimes they exert political efforts in alliance with other
groups sincerely interested in peace and justice. In the Hungry
World one of the principal instruments through which communism seeks to work is nationalism.

Sophisticated communists claim that they are socialists of a
higher degree. Socialists and communists alike, they claim,
believe in the public ownership and operation of the means of
production and distribution; the difference is that whereas under
socialism people are paid for what they produce, under communism the state withers away, leaving a classless society ruled
by the Marxian principle "from each according to his abilities,
to each according to his needs." This myth is deliberately misleading. Though it is a quotation from one of socialism's founding fathers, it has nothing to do with reality.

In the Soviet Union, where the communists have been in
power for forty-one years, wage differentials are greater than
in the United States, and all wages are based on performance
rather than need; the state is oppressively strong and shows no

signs of withering away, while the individual citizens and the collective public have surrendered control of the economy to a small self-perpetuating communist oligarchy.

Socialism

Socialism is a system of society in which the public, operating through a more or less representative state, exercises varying degrees of ownership and control over the means of production and distribution. Doctrinal socialists hold that such controls are virtues to be striven for. Many others do not think of such controls as "socialist" at all, but rather, regard them as unwanted children of modern technology.

Controls are today being applied in varying degrees throughout the entire world. Several years ago I heard Norman Thomas remark that, as Socialist candidate for President of the United States in the 1920's, he would not have dared advocate a federal housing law as "socialist" as that supported in the Senate in 1948 by Robert Taft. From the multi-billion-dollar United States Atomic Energy Commission through the nationalized coal industry in Britain, state-owned railroads in West Germany, Turkey's virtual state monopoly of foreign trade, India's comprehensive Five Year Plan to President Ngo Dinh Diem's new state-owned cement and textile industries, one measure of control after another has been instituted in the non-Communist world.

The degree of this public control can be measured by comparing the size of the public and private sectors in an economy. This measure, incidentally, is meaningless in the Soviet economy because there the public has no control over the state, and there is thus literally no public sector. The degree of socialism in the Soviet Union is thus smaller than in the United States. To illustrate this important point: There is far more public control over the General Motors Corporation than over the Magnitogorsk Metallurgical Plant. It is exercised through dispersed stock ownership, through such government organs as the Securities and Exchange Commission, the Interstate Commerce Commission, and the directors of Internal Revenue, and through trade unions over which GM has no control. No equivalent controls operate in Magnitogorsk, which is run directly and exclusively by a self-perpetuating and unrepresentative oligarchy, the Communist party.

Two generations ago, when traveling along a road, a man passed left or right, he regulated his starts and stops and speeds to his own taste. Today he is overwhelmed with traffic lights, stop signs, no-parking signs, one-way streets, minimum and maximum speeds. These measures are generally recognized as necessary to protect the community against the irresponsible misuse of modern vehicles. Productive forces embodied by the modern factory, the separation of many workers from the ownership of the means of production, and the concentration of enormous economic power in a few individual and corporate hands have rendered similarly necessary the stop signs and other restrictions administered by governmental organizations from the SEC in Washington to its thousands of counterparts in other countries.

To associate this need for controls with Marx, Engels, Lenin, and Stalin by calling it "socialism" is as misleading and illogical as it would be to accuse a cardinal of communist sympathies because he wears a red hat.

But millions of men and women in the Hungry World juxtapose socialism and capitalism, while equating the latter with colonialism, which they blame for their poverty and humiliating lack of freedom. And indeed, most nineteenth-century colonialists were capitalists, investing surplus capital in enterprises in dependent areas and trying to realize from these investments a maximum profit squeezed from the local populace by a combination of economic, political, and military pressures.

Upon achieving political independence, most retarded countries find themselves faced with immediate problems—large numbers of landless and debt-ridden peasants, armies of unemployed, and a desperate shortage of capital. In most cases, there is no middle class, so that business initiative has to come from the government. In most retarded countries there are no local industrialists, engineers, or managers with experience or the capital or the psychology to develop a free-enterprise economy. The government is forced not only to control the economy but to own and operate it.

Thus when an Indonesian today says he is a socialist or when we examine the political parties of Burma and find that all are dedicated to governmental ownership and operation of huge sectors of the economy, these Asians may simply be finding pragmatic solutions to economic and human problems inherited from generations of "capitalist-colonialism."

In newly developed countries like Mexico, Japan, the Philippines, Singapore, and Israel, although both the latter have socialist governments, we find a healthy degree of private enterprise and business initiative. As others acquire experience and accumulate savings, they may lose their current dependence on their governments, whose role will then be modified from one of outright ownership and operation to one of guidance and control, *if* the people of these nations retain their political freedom and do not allow themselves to be enslaved by the self-perpetuating bureaucracy of a communist state.

Therefore, these four magic words—colonialism, nationalism, communism, socialism—lie at the heart of the social and economic chemistry that is so rapidly changing the Hungry World. Their substance and interpretation underlie our competition with the Russians for the minds and allegiances of most of our fellow men.

Two ⊘ *Sights and Sounds and Smells*

During five consecutive years, I traveled the Hungry World. Nearly half a million miles by air and sea, by road and river, watching and listening. Often with my wife, sometimes alone, I groped first for the right questions, then for answers.

In every capital I tried to see someone in the government, someone from the opposition; a banker and a businessman or two, a teacher, a trade-union leader, a doctor or an engineer, a priest, mullah, or missionary. I called, of course, on diplomatic representatives, including the Russians where they were in evidence. Everywhere I saw local editors and foreign correspondents from other lands. Everywhere I sought, and sometimes found, philosophers. Then in every country I tried to see some enterprise important to the local people: an oil field, a tin mine, a rubber plantation, a steel mill.

Periodically, I set down on paper such answers as I had found. These notes of substance, contrast, and comparison formed the material for five reports to my publisher. As I worked over these reports, the polemic theses of this book took shape.

Latin America

In a busy suburb of Cali, Colombia, I stood in awe before the imposing Church of the Eucharist, a huge cathedral dome on

25

eight reinforced-concrete columns, towering above the muddy muddled streets. Under the dome huddled a wooden shack in which Mass was daily said. The cathedral was built from the top down, and after putting up the roof, the builders had run out of money.

The church at Cali became a symbol of the imbalance of performance, the confusion of aims and means and timing not only in Colombia but from the Rio Grande to the Horn. As I traveled among our nearly 200 million Latin neighbors, the influence of this symbol was always present.

More than half of our Latin neighbors are illiterate, millions of them undernourished and poorly housed; they lack roads and bridges, stable currencies and adequate sources of food. Yet they have gone ahead with some of the world's most spectacular and beautiful architecture; they have built four modern steel mills, a magnificent Municipal Center in Caracas, admirable university campuses like that in Mexico City, several of the world's most beautiful and modern airports like that outside Buenos Aires, and created some of the world's best modern art.

Why have our neighbors built their houses from the roof down? Perhaps Latin America's explosive population-increase rate—nearly 3 per cent a year, by far the highest in the world—keeps them constantly off balance in their desperate attempts to keep production ahead of reproduction. Perhaps this is one of the reasons for their apparent political instability.

I pursued this hypothesis as I traveled through the tiny tense republics of Central America, where mestizos moil midst the ruins of old Mayan and Tultec civilizations which had drunk and fought their way to steep decline before the conquistadors came with their guns and horses, their alien god, and their unslaked thirst for gold. And their political heirs, the Samosas and Trujillos, myopic worshipers of pure power, far from knowing answers, could not even perceive the questions.

Castillo Armas, then President of a still-seething Guatemala, was wading courageously through the mire left by an abortive

Marxist revolution. He had eyes for little more. "Pepe" Figueras, well-meaning and personable President of Costa Rica, along with several local trade-union leaders, did have some idea of the relation between production and consumption and economic development, but most of the spider waist of our hemisphere seemed as capricious and unthinking as its volcanoes.

I went on down the coast, sniffing at the senseless dictatorship of Rojas Penilla, leavened by the wisdom of Alberto Lleras Camargo, one of the hemisphere's truly great. I explored for one steamy weekend the prolific lowlands near Guayaquil, so sharply contrasted by austere severity as reflected in the impressive Casa de la Cultura Equadoriana of upland Quito.

In sophisticated and slum-scarred Lima, I was a visitor in the fabled mansion of a wealthy antiquarian and recluse, Don Pedro de la Osma, who had spent his life and an immense fortune on a collection of Cuzco art unequaled by any museum, a man living wholly in the sixteenth century, unaware of and uninterested in politics, economics, in the lives of the miserable Aymara Indians, descendants of the ancient Incas, who labored in his metal mines.

In Lima I asked questions of some of the continent's most powerful publishers, presidential aspirant Don Pedro Beltran, and the numerous and energetic members of the Miro Quesada family, at least one of whom, Paco, professor of philosophy in the hemisphere's oldest university, knew the questions, and perhaps some answers.

Then I flew up over the dizzy mountains to Cuzco and Machu Picchu to gape at the mute remnants of what had been our hemisphere's most benign and reasonable civilization until illiterate ruffian Francisco Pizarro came to loot and lie and rape into being the present poor remnants of so proud a past.

In Bolivia, when my wife and I caught our breath, we wondered why the rugged Quechuas stayed up on their arid altiplano, mining tin at a loss, ignoring the fertile virgin valleys, and how long it would take the noisy revolution to run the country into bankruptcy, and what would happen then. Finding no answers, we went on to the civilized, temperate south, Chile and Argentina and Uruguay, whose European population remains unblended with the Indian and Negro, so much in evidence farther north. Here literate and diligent men and women, who should have known better, succumbed to the grinding dictatorship of Juan Perón, whose overthrow we saw in midair. Here the debilitating influence of the welfare state and of irresponsibility had led Uruguay to crisis; while crippling inflation, seemingly arranged by some of the continent's most sophisticated economists in Santiago, had brought Chile to the verge of bankruptcy.

The temperate south left us with a new doubt: did literacy, relative economic well-being, and absence from racial tensions and hostilities lead to effective democracy? Could democracy avoid breeding monsters even in fertile soil? We passed cultured and urbane evenings in gracious homes. We flew over the hemisphere's crowning mountain majesty, Aconcagua, while in a seat across the aisle a quiet girl penciled marginal notes in the *Odyssey*; we sampled some of the world's most justly famous beef and wine. But we heard no answers, except perhaps the implicit and unspoken axiom which so bemused Thucydides (and is still so poorly understood in much of the United States): that an island of relative affluence and political freedom in a sea of slaves and savages tends to succumb to the poisons in the sullied air even if it escapes the swords and arrows of the barbarians.

In Brazil we saw some answers acted out in heavy-shouldered, raucous, healthy cities like São Paulo, where economic growth was explosive and capital so short that banks paid 5 per cent on checking accounts and short-term money was unobtainable at 20 per cent. Here miscegenation, as it seems to do in all multiracial societies, had melted the grinning, busy millions into a friendly neutral brown, while the unscratched wealth of the world's second largest nation beckoned enterprise toward quick reward. But political short circuits and the shortage of capital have kept their economy permanently off balance. Brazil was spending $100 million a year for grain which could have been effectively raised in Brazil and $200 million on petroleum products, although Brazil is conceded by nearly all competent geologists to have an immense oil potential. These two items consume nearly all the foreign exchange Brazil receives from its coffee exports and leaves the country dry of dollars for the Cadillacs and air conditioners which the country's *nouveau riche* so cherishes. We inspected the trim new steel mill at Volta Redonda and the grim Favella—squatter settlements poxed across the face of every city—and tried in vain to twist stumbling Spanish into Portuguese.

Then for twelve grinding hours over the endless jungle to Venezuela, that burly hybrid with Miami's glitter and the explosive energy of Texas. The bellboy at the Tamanaco sniffed indifferently at a fifty-cent tip.

The oil fields throbbed with drive and, also, social progress through the community integration program. But thought was stifled by Jimenez and his ubiquitous police, while misery and destitution showed everywhere through the cracks and holes in Latin America's statistically most affluent economy.

THE WHY OF UNSTABILITY

Why, in a century of independence, had our neighbors not succeeded in establishing stable institutions? Why had all but four of the twenty Latin lands we visited suffered extralegal changes of government during the past generation, while the United States and Canada had maintained relative stability and order?

First: racial heterogeniety. Whereas the Indians north of the Rio Grande were few, warlike, and independent, who fought and lost and all but disappeared, Latin America's Indians were numerous, accustomed to work and to authority. So the conquistadors baptized them and put them to work mining gold and raising the mestizos, cholos, and latinos who soon made up the bulk of the population. To increase the confusion, several million African slaves were imported. Miscegenation was immediate, and soon Latin America, except for the extreme south, was peopled by brown-skinned men and women with virtually no roots or traditions, whose behavior was determined by arbitrary authority cruelly enforced and reluctantly accepted. That such men and women could not be expected to establish stable institutions immediately was obvious.

Then there was history. For 300 years—from about 1500 until about 1800—Latin America had been extremely stable. While the Reformation, the Renaissance, the French Revolution, and the Industrial Revolution shook Western Europe, Spain and Portugal protected their subjects at home and in the colonies from new ideas and change—one king, one language, one church, one centralized bureaucracy untempered by any local government.

The United States (and Canada) experienced the Renaissance and the Reformation prenatally, later embodied in their own development many of the ideas of the French Revolution, and actually helped spearhead the Industrial Revolution. All this while Latin America remained stable and changeless.

Then in a short space of time the Spanish and Portuguese empires disintegrated, and Latin America, cast loose, tried to assimilate three centuries of change along with the newer problems raised by Marx and Lenin. The task, at best forbidding, was complicated by the almost complete lack of any traditions of local self-government such as could be found in any African village. As one Latin American statesman put it to me: "All Thomas Jefferson had to do was to describe a historic fact—that the American colonies were and had been since about 1600 self-governing from the village level up. In Latin America we had virtually no self-government on any level until the nineteenth century. To this day presidents appoint provincial governors, who in turn appoint mayors of cities and villages. We still use the administrative system taken over from the Spanish and the Portuguese...."

Latin America's nations had never really existed. After their haphazard rebellions against Spain and Portugal they declared themselves republics but often shortly became dictatorships run by corrupt and venal men with little sense of social responsibility, men who enriched themselves as best they could until ousted by revolution in favor of other dictators, no better.

These problems in government were summed up for me by philosopher (and now President of Colombia) Camargo as follows:

We are impatient. Frequently we do not understand that before we can become consumers we must become producers. When we do understand this, we lack the capital. We see that our North American neighbors have machines and are rich. Very well, we say, we shall get machines and be rich. When wiser men tell us that we must first build schools, learn to read and write, to elect effective local governments, to accumulate the capital to buy the machines, and acquire the knowledge to use them, it seems to many of us that all this is useless red tape.

Add to this an irrational land-tenure system inherited from those early days of grab and keep and the atrophied corruption of a church too long unchallenged in its position of monopoly. Quite aside from the poverty and illiteracy so prevalent and oppressive, it would have been surprising indeed if stable democratic institutions had emerged among our Latin neighbors to the south.

Asia

Asia is a big part of the Hungry World. My first Asian journey was to India, Ceylon, and Pakistan, where human poverty and misery achieve a mass unmatched in any other part of the world.

INDIA

In Calcutta's torrid, dusty streets I have seen the people wrapped in rags, sleeping sometimes on wooden cots or reed mattresses, rising early to squat at the curb, urinate, and wash their teeth with their fingers. Cows were everywhere, flocks of sheep and goats abundant; huge water buffaloes lumbered through the streets, while cars swerved, screeching.

Bombay seemed less oppressive. Delicate, ascetic Chief Minister Morarji Desai, now India's Finance Minister, explained to me the process through which he, a pacifist, vegetarian, seeker for truth and right, could use his police to keep order, banish the holy cows to the suburbs, and force the sprawling city into some semblance of order.

In Madras I have watched machinery arriving from every corner of both worlds for transshipment to southern India's new industrial cities by lorry, oxcart, plane, and rail. I have tramped over the fertile fields of a modest farmer whose thirteen acres absorbed the labor of a dozen men and in turn paid them the bare subsistence that is the best the rural Indian can expect.

Here in southern India and in the north and west I have watched community development projects slowly changing the face of India by getting the peasants up off their patient haunches to dig wells, mend roads, and build schools with materials provided by the government. The organizers of this movement were in most cases products of the training schools set up by the Ford Foundation in co-operation with India's dynamic director of community development, S. K. Dey, in one of the most effective of all the American aid projects.

In Vizagapatam I have seen an oil refinery, and in Bhilai and Jamshedpur I have shouldered among the sweating Sikh steel and construction workers of two million-ton plants being built in ostentatious competition by Americans and Russians. The Ganges, the Taj, the Red Fort were all they are supposed to be; Kashmir was far more, a real enchanted vale, its terraced gardens and fragile beauty somehow marred by the memory of the violence so often visited on this Asian Eden and still today so near the shimmering surface.

When my wife and I reached New Delhi the second time, I had been benumbed, as had so many before me, immunized against the vultures picking at the dying and the dead, the streams of refugees passing each other in their frightened flight from violences and hunger, the sad pride with which the young and diligent pointed to their brave efforts to modernize a country buried under the weight of its own history, India's special problem.

In repeated talks with some of Asia's and the world's most civilized men I looked for answers: Why was the land so backward? Why only now, after five thousand years of flood and drought, was the Bhakra Dam being built? Why did scores of millions of "unemployed" squat in squalid idleness while their wives scratched a few vegetables from the exhausted soil and nursed the naked scabby children they begot?

THE WEIGHT OF HISTORY

About 1600 B.C. the Aryan invasions of India began. We do not know just who the Aryans were except that they were fair-skinned and came from the north, possibly from what is now Russia, or even Germany. Over the mountains in the Indus Valley the invaders found an ancient and perhaps then already-decadent Dravidian culture, which they overwhelmed. Some of the dark-skinned Dravidians probably fled southward and eastward, where they enslaved the black-skinned aborigines who dwelt there. Others probably remained and were enslaved by the invaders, whom they gradually absorbed. This process may have lasted 500 years, and during it the caste system crystallized, in part to prevent the miscegenation which, nevertheless, took place, and partly as a sort of social security system.

The Indians (and the Ceylonese) are tormented by a resultant color consciousness. The Indian tends to look up to those lighter than himself and down at those darker. Justice, tyranny, exploitation—all exist for the Indian essentially in color terms.

Though the caste system has now legally been abolished, color is still of great importance. One example is the premarital inspections which still precede betrothals in most Indian communities. The prospective groom's father and another relative or adviser go to the girl and subject her to scrutiny, in which the color of her skin is a major factor. Sometimes the family of a dark-skinned bride find a lighter substitute for the inspection, and not infrequently such conspiracies wind up in courts of law.

Nehru, when I saw him in his neat, simple office, was optimistic about the caste system:

> It is definitely breaking down. In industry and indeed among most of our city dwellers, it has virtually disappeared, except perhaps with regard to marriage. Other things have come to replace it in the minds of the people. The Five Year Plan and everything involved in it. . . .

Nehru's optimism was inspiring, but other evidence convinced me that both caste and color neurosis will long plague India along with other atavisms.

IS REALITY REAL OR RELEVANT?

For a hundred generations of Indians sweating under the mesmerizing blaze of the Indian sun, fact and fancy, story and reality have become blurred; and for many, measured magnitudes and economic facts, budgets and bovine mortality are unreal or certainly unimportant.

Hindu scriptural epics, the lives and loves of their many gods and goddesses, some with many arms and legs, others with elephants' trunks, are so real to many Indians that they are satisfied to live only in this mythological realm, ignoring the sordid world about them.

As Hinduism ossified in recent years, its myths and foibles survive today as absurd anachronisms, such as suttee—the suicide of the widow on her husband's funeral pyre.

The Indians are often conscious of this problem. Deploring his countrymen's leanings to fantasy, Jawaharlal Nehru wrote:

The ignoring of history had evil consequences which pursue us still. It produced a vagueness of outlook, a divorce from life as it is, a credulity, a wooliness of the mind. . . . [The Indian mind] was uncritical where fact was concerned, perhaps because it did not attach much importance to fact as such. . . .

A Jamshedpur steel-mill engineer told me:

We have difficulties, particularly with our younger engineers, in achieving exactitude. We tell a man to keep a furnace at 124°. Then we come around in an hour and find it 130°. The young man shrugs at our indignation. "It's hot, is it not?"

Once in northern India we were driving with a Sikh chauffeur, a literate man who had put in several years in the army under British officers, a punctual and efficient driver. We had decided to drive to Amritsar and I asked Singh how far it was. "Far, Sahib," he said. "How many miles?" I asked. He shrugged. "We should not try to drive it in the morning." I asked again how many miles it was. Again I got no answer. Finally, after ten minutes I learned that Singh did not know how many miles it was, nor was he interested in finding out. It was unimportant, even irrelevant to our travel plans. The important things were the weather, the state of the road, the fact that I had a slight cold, and probably how Singh himself felt. To make travel plans on the basis of a mere measurement, so and so many miles, seemed to Singh pedantic and stupid.

And indeed it is only with the utmost difficulty that many Indians can bring themselves to what we would call rational attitudes. To persuade the Indians of the desirability of preventing the Communist party from winning an election or putting the unemployed to work is often all but impossible.

Yet some Indians have achieved a perception and logic as keen as any I ever encountered. One of the most striking was

Minoo Masani, a Parsi businessman and politician, writer and philosopher, with whom I spent a number of fascinating hours. Minoo visited the Soviet Union in the thirties and at one time was a fellow traveler of sorts. Here is a succinct, critical evaluation of Indian neutralism in the light of Soviet reality that he offered over dinner one evening:

The French Revolution was a rather crude transition from feudalism to capitalism. Having achieved this result, it underwent the usual modifications; made its peace with other contemporary sociologies; was sanctified, buried, and ossified. The new business class accumulated capital by exploiting labor and used it to build industries at home and abroad.

The Russians in 1917 were in a position roughly similar to that of the French in 1789. And the revolution was essentially the same. It overthrew Russian feudalism and inaugurated Russian capitalism —which proceeded to industrialize, modernize, exploit, discipline, and regiment Russian workers and peasants with more brutality by far than that employed by any past capitalistic class anywhere. There was some new "socialist" nomenclature; and some liberals were misled into thinking that the new Soviet ruling class was something other than what it was; but it is now painfully clear that the Russian Revolution of 1917 introduced a nationalist state capitalism in the Soviet Union, which for thirty-five years built up the strength of the country, defeated its foreign enemies, lined up likely foreign allies, formulated and stylized its ideology—and accumulated large quantities of what Marx would have called capital or accumulated surplus value, in an immense industrialized economy, control of which was tightly held and bitterly fought for by a small group of a few thousand leading Communists.

In the meantime, in the West the struggle of men for freedom proceeded apace. Trade unions fought for and won better working conditions. Civil rights were likewise won and guaranteed; and the entire sociology of the West changed gradually in the direction that Marx had predicted society would go through revolution. In Russia, where the revolution had "succeeded," all the evils, like the extraction of surplus value from the working classes down to the last of their ability to produce it and go on working the next day, were practiced with a consistency and a brutality unequaled in the world until the Chinese Revolution succeeded in 1950.

Now perhaps this struggle for freedom is beginning in the Soviet Union. Perhaps the insurrections in Posnan and East Germany are the equivalent of the Chartist movement in the West, and will eventually lead to the freedom of the working people in the Soviet area and to the establishment of a rule of humanity and law. The struggle will probably be long and bitter.

But during this period, what "neutralism" can there be? What should Indians be "neutral" between? Why should we consider the U.S.S.R. and the United States equal evils; or, worse, why should we consider the Soviet Union "right" and the United States as imperialistic? Yet this is Nehru's policy.

Yet Masani himself on some issues was as far from being rational or logical as was the object of his ire—Jawaharlal Nehru.

Most of the conversation I had with Nehru was devoted to the Five Year Plan. Figures, percentages, budgets, estimates flowed from his lips in a steady and impressive stream. Yet when I mentioned Kashmir his logic grew unhinged, and his conversation became all but irrational.

When I raised the key question of the future of democracy, Nehru answered with a vagueness he himself bitterly criticized in others. I was left to conclude that if democracy survived in India, it would be in great measure thanks to the efforts of others rather than as a result of rational and provident planning by the Indians themselves.

CEYLON

Ceylon is a tiny India, with similar characteristics more deeply etched. The food is spicier, the caste consciousness more intense, the Communist party proportionately stronger and better led, linguistic conflicts more explosive. I sought wisdom in a Buddhist monastery, and with my wife and daughter tramped around exquisite Kandy, the ancient capital. We heard out hour-long expressions against the Portuguese, Dutch, and British invaders, who in sequence had plundered the verdant island and sought to exploit its people. Now independent but enmeshed with trade agreements with mainland China and contemplating new ties with the Soviet Union, Ceylon seemed naïvely hopeful. "Russia has never had colonies. The Communist countries want trade, and so do we. The British still want bases, and the Americans want their concessions and do not allow us to use their economic aid to buy Soviet machines."

I had no reply, except to wonder verbally whether the next election would bring more Communists to positions of authority. "Yes," I was told by local observers, and the next year's elections bore out the opinion.

PAKISTAN

We spent but a week in Karachi—a city swarming with refugees and acid threats against the "decadent" Indians. "We will show them, as soon as we get a few more American arms . . ." When I suggested that the arms were intended to defend the country against Soviet aggression, I often saw a look of pained surprise, and then heard an earnest, "Oh, but you don't understand about Kashmir and the Indian control of all our rivers' headwaters."

The more I studied Pakistan's economic position, the less confidence I felt in the country's physical survival. For it is not really a nation but rather two nations, separated by a thousand miles of hostile territory, without direct communications. East and West Pakistan speak different languages, have unconnected economies, and are basically divergent in race and tradition. They are tied together only by their Moslem faith. This lack of unity alone, aside from other pressing problems, has made it questionable whether Pakistan will long survive as a nation.

In addition to its running vendetta with India, Pakistan has a territorial conflict with its northern neighbor. The issue is Pushtoonistan, a long tongue of land running from the Afghan border southward to the sea. Pakistan considers Pushtoonistan part of its sovereign territory. The Afghans want Pushtoonistan to have its own autonomous government. In fact, this area is inhabited by fierce tribesmen closely related to the Afghans by blood (the King of Afghanistan is a Pushtoon) but separated from Afghanistan and incorporated into the Northwest Frontier Provinces of British India in 1894. In 1955 the Pakistanis closed the Afghan frontier for five months, thereby denying Afghanistan access to the sea through Pakistan, a route over which 80 per cent of Afghanistan's foreign trade had traditionally moved. The Soviet Union thereupon stepped into the situation by supplying Afghanistan with essential imports at artificially low prices, supplying markets for Afghan exports, and opening for Afghanistan's trade a new transit route through the Soviet Union to the Black Sea.

Although the United States has kept out of the Pushtoonistan issue, Pakistan is our ally; the Afghans feel, therefore, that we are against them, while the Pakistanis reproach us with lack of enthusiasm in their support.

AFGHANISTAN

The Afghans, of course, have been the recipient of a good part of Moscow's ruble diplomacy. The mountainous kingdom, with its twelve million illiterate Moslem tribesmen, has no political parties and virtually no press. Afghanistan's particular problem is that the whole show of government is a family affair. Prime Minister Prince Daud, first cousin to the King, runs a taut police state. The Prince's brother is Minister of Foreign Affairs, and other high administrative posts are in the hands of other relatives. The Parliament consists of a Senate with fifty members, appointed for life by the King, and a National Assembly of 171 "elected" members, but power rests pretty much with the King and the Prime Minister and the rest of the royal family. For the foreseeable future there can be no serious talk of democracy in Afghanistan. This reality fits in perfectly with the plans of Soviet strategists, anxious to make common cause with "healthy nationalist movements" against "Wall Street imperialists and their Asian agents."

East Asia

I traveled alone to East Asia, flying southward from Korea, in a majestic arch around the periphery of Communist China, to Burma. Only a few years ago the whole area was conquered and herded by Japan into its Greater East Asia Co-Prosperity Sphere. Now its principal preoccupation has again become its ancient problem—China.

During the whole huge trek, month after weary month, I was conscious of the ever-pressing Chinese. In grim Korea the entire economy was harnessed to the world's fourth largest land army, stationed, with four United States divisions, along the ragged pitted front, facing the Chinese "volunteers." Though the island-born Japanese and Filipinos felt relatively safe from Chinese aggression, they were still obsessed with the nearness of the world's most populous nation and its ultimate importance to trade.

Sweeping down on the surf-laced Ryukyus from twenty thousand feet, I found Okinawa, a tiny enclave of America, preoccupied with preparations to forestall or defeat the Chicom's expected aggression.

Formosa and Hong Kong, technically parts of China, were obsessed with Chinese affairs, and I found by no means everyone on these two strategic archipelagos supporting Chiang's nationalist regime.

In Saigon I was struck by *la présence française*, so much discussed and so little felt in North Africa, but so clearly visible at every hand in what was only recently a rebellious French colony. Phnom Penh was relaxed and friendly, while Vientiane was completely disarming, though China's shadow lay heavily on both Cambodia and Laos.

On down the coast I spent a week in Singapore and several

days in K.L., as the Malayans call their steaming capital of Kuala Lumpur. These now separate and independent parts of what was the Straits Settlements were prosperous and vigorous, but more than half their total population was ethnically Chinese. Though courageous local leaders like Singapore's Chief Minister Lim Yew Hok talked confidently of resisting Communist aggression, he and most of the other local Chinese with whom I talked were frankly proud of the achievements of what they called the "New China."

I found Bangkok the most pleasant city in the Orient and the Thais the most subtle and flexible of its people. But it was not difficult to see the failings of the tender Thai democracy functioning under a constitution written with the help of several American professors. And, indeed, it was not many months after my visit that a coup brought down the government and established what could only be called a military dictatorship.

Rangoon was the disorderly capital of a badly disordered Burma, plagued by a three-way civil war in which Karen nationalists, two different stripes of Communists (one pro-Moscow, the other pro-Peking), and a number of honest, nonpolitical bandits controlled large parts of the country in defiance of the government, which talked about progressive socialism, but in fact had still not restored the economy or the vital rice crop to prewar levels.

From a number of urbane British-trained government officials and from Ed Law Yone, one of Asia's ablest journalists, I got a pessimistic picture of a harassed nation under constant threat of a Chinese invasion, which neither the Burmese themselves nor anyone else could stop if the Chicoms decided to push through to their "Trieste" and the warm water of the Bay of Bengal. Internally, various legal and illegal Communist parties and the fronts through which they operated seemed likely to take over within a year or two unless some new strong man took power.

Right around the rim of Asia I found men's main preoccupation was China. Only in Indonesia did China seem a little more remote.

The Indonesians now number close to ninety million, and they live on several thousand islands scattered in a sea the size of North America. I visited the two most important, Java and Sumatra, and talked at length with the inimitable President Sukarno, his Prime Minister Djuanda, and with many political leaders and technicians as well as foreign observers. Near Sumatra's junglebound Pakanbaru I tramped and drove over one of Asia's richest oil fields; I talked with the separatist leaders and heard the Sumatran claims for independence exchanged with equally vehement Javanese demands for unity. I went over the balance sheets of a nation in a state of net disinvestment and talked to Javanese farmers who called themselves Communists because economic disintegration had left them without a living and without hope. I talked with a number of Chinese, members of the three-million-strong Chinese colony, most of them Indonesian born, who control so much of the archipelago's business and so many of whom send their sons to mainland schools.

Why has China so dominated this whole area? In the comfortable home of oil executive friends I found a fine library on East Asia, through which I leafed my way for several days looking for an answer.

THE ANCIENT FOE

Until about 1000 B.C. Indian influence seemed to predominate in the Golden Peninsula. But about that time China overtook India and began to press outward in all directions, trading, conquering, exacting tribute.

Chinese pressures on Korea and Japan go back beyond any written record. During the first millennium B.C. China pushed southward, finding primitive Australasians emerging from neolithic culture and beginning to cultivate the soil. China conquered and absorbed the northern part of what is now Viet-Nam. Further southward the Chinese did not extend political authority. But massive migrations from Yunnan produced an infusion of Chinese blood and culture into the whole peninsula, over whose youthful warring little states China exercised "suzerainty," collecting periodic tribute and keeping a kind of unsettled order by periodic military expeditions. About the first century A.D. the Chinese reached Indonesia, inhabited by simple people called K'un-lun by the Chinese and Dvipantara by the Indians—People of the Islands. At about the same time the Chinese crossed the mountains and invaded Burma and parts of Bengal.

From then on and for some fifteen centuries, China exercised its suzerainty over that huge area of the world extending from Kamchatka to New Guinea to Bengal. Chinese sailors went farther and established posts as far away as Madagascar, over which China at one time claimed suzerainty. At several points, when China's government was most effective, as it was under the Khans, the Chinese mainland mothered massive invasions which pushed inland armies into Europe and large navies into Indonesia.

Of course China had problems. The Khmers and Chams and Shans and Burmese rebelled, the Thais made deals, and the Viet-Namese remained a restive undigested people like the Irish or the Basques. One of the greatest challenges to China came from an Indonesian King of Palembang, who cut off the noses of a Chinese deputation and fought the subsequent punitive expedition so effectively that his son, Prince Vijaya, was able to found the Majapahit state which existed for nearly three centuries in periodic defiance of China, collecting tribute on its own from its satellites in Java and Sumatra. But even Majapahit paid occasional tribute to China and along with the entire Orient spent much of its time and energy absorbing, resisting, or fighting Chinese aggression.

Then there came a series of startling changes. In a spectacular wave of religious proselytization Moslem missionaries converted much of Southeast Asia to Islam, thereby challenging, in effect, the complaisant Chinese, whose religious tolerance amounted almost to atheism. At almost the same time the Europeans made their appearance—first the Portuguese, followed shortly by the Spaniards, Dutch, and British. Armed with improved weapons, the Europeans did something the Chinese had never done—they established forts and manned them permanently. By the seventeenth century the Europeans were well established in India, Ceylon, Indonesia, and up the coast to China. During the next two centuries they pushed steadily on, opening up Japan, and even invading and partitioning China itself. They traded, made converts to Christianity, suppressed rebellions, established schools, built factories and roads. They also fought with one another.

The question arises: Why did the Chinese allow these despised alien barbarians to take over, without a fight, an area they had dominated for two thousand years? The answer probably lies in the internal weakness of China after the fall of the Mings, plus the impetus of the Industrial Revolution in Europe.

In any case, for a century of uninhibited colonialism, the Europeans dominated the Orient, trading, ruling, looting, building, exploiting, hated and feared by most Asians, fawned over by their local puppets.

In two ways they prepared their own destruction. They trained a local intelligentsia, a local native elite, which was bound at some point to try to take back control of its country. Second, they fought unceasingly among themselves, war after war, culminating in World War II, when the white man was driven from most of the Orient by the Japanese, and though Japan lost the war, everyone in the Orient knew that the period of white colonialism was over. And indeed it was. Within a decade *merdeka* came to the entire area, while in 1950 the Europeans were driven from the Chinese mainland. The fact that the Communist government of Peking executed the eviction was, I think, accidental. More relevant was that a strong Chinese government was reasserting its historic position. Had the Nationalist government consolidated its power over the mainland of China and become a strong and effective central authority, it would have expelled the foreigners from the Orient with as much vigor. Indeed, Sir Alexander Grantham, then Governor of Hong Kong, told me he had had far more trouble with the Nationalists from 1945 until 1949 than with the Communists for the next seven years.

I am not belittling the importance of the Communist victory in China nor trying to equate the Communist and Nationalist governments. But I am convinced that the central fact is the reassertion of China's historic domination of the Orient, leaving thoughtful Asians to brace themselves to take up again their ancient struggle with their old opponents, the Chinese.

Like Shakespeare's Idiot, the white man had strutted his brief moment across an alien stage and disappeared, leaving the old actors and stage hands to take over again.

This historical inevitability was rendered the more likely by the presence throughout the Orient of some fourteen million overseas Chinese, an advance guard and potential fifth column.

THE OVERSEAS CHINESE

The biggest single Chinese community outside China itself is in Thailand, where 3.5 million Chinese, most of them born and raised there, dominate the retail trade and small-scale banking of the country. These Chinese, who represent more than one-eighth of the country's population, exert great influence in the professions and foreign trade as well.

The next important Chinese community is in Malaya, whose three million Chinese constitute nearly half the population. Hong Kong's 2.5 million Chinese make up 90 per cent of the population of the crown colony. In Indonesia roughly three million Chinese exercise monopoly control over small trade and some small industry. In Viet-Nam, there are about one million Chinese; in Cambodia, about 400,000; in Laos, 30,000.

One of the most difficult Chinese communities to evaluate is that in the Philippines. It probably numbers half a million, although official estimates are much smaller. The 500,000 Chinese in Burma are less important than a similar group in other countries might be because they are balanced by a competitive minority, the Indians. Other contingents of overseas Chinese include: 900,000 in Singapore—they constitute an overwhelming majority of the population of the city—125,000 in the United States, about 200,000 in Latin America, some 50,000 in Hawaii, and 38,000 in Japan.

The Chinese Nationalist government, of course, pays great attention to the overseas Chinese, tries to maintain contact with them and keep them informed.

On its side the Chinese Communist government has designated two organs, one state and one party, to study, penetrate, and utilize the overseas Chinese. At low or no cost they furnish books and moving pictures to overseas Chinese clubs and other groups; they subsidize schools; they furnish textbooks and in some cases teachers. They publish magazines and newspapers. They engage in many different kinds of economic subsidy to individuals and groups. Every year several thousand overseas Chinese are invited to go to China to study with all expenses paid.

Underlying this conflict for the sympathy and allegiance of the overseas Chinese is the basic fact that these communities do not assimilate. For many years they have been living, seeking fortunes and new lives outside the frontiers of their overcrowded motherland. Yet they have remained Chinese in race, language, customs, and in their loyalties and obligations. These *tsai shen yeh*, or "gods of fortune" as they call themselves, rarely intermarry with the natives of the countries where they live. I asked a number of overseas Chinese in many parts of Southeast Asia why this was so and received one simple answer: "We feel ourselves superior."

One Chinese journalist, a fourth generation Indonesian citizen, told me: "If my daughter married an Indonesian, I would be disappointed."

In Hong Kong a Chinese girl told me that if she really fell in love and the man were economically and professionally suitable, she might marry an American or even an Englishman but certainly not a Japanese, Filipino, Malayan, or Indonesian.

The overseas Chinese have two great assets of which they have made full use in carving out for themselves positions of importance and security in the countries where they lived. In the first place, they work indefatigably. Second, they stick together.

By doing these two things, they have made themselves the object of envy and hatred on the part of other Asians, very much as did the Jews in Central Europe and for the same reasons. The Chinese shops open first and close last. The proprietor will always let good customers have a bit of this and that on credit. When he is in trouble—sickness, misfortune, bankruptcy—other Chinese help him out.

There is one significant difference between the position of the Jews in Europe and the overseas Chinese in Asia. The population of Israel is 1,800,000. The population of China is over 600,000,000.

Dutch and French colonial governments long favored the Chinese minority in their colonies against the native majority, much as the French used the Jews in the largely Moslem Algeria. Since World War II, as country after country in Southeast Asia won its independence, the new governments proceeded to pass official legislation—reminiscent of the anti-Jewish regulations in Czarist Russia or the unofficial restrictions limiting Jewish entry into many American medical and law schools—barring the Chinese from engaging in certain professions.

As I traveled throughout Southeast Asia, I found that Communist influence was increasing among the overseas Chinese. The reasons for this are clear. In those countries where they are able to operate, the Chinese Communists are making major economic as well as political efforts. They are offering favorable credit terms to overseas Chinese importing mainland sewing machines, bicycles, thermos jugs, textiles, and assorted *chinoiseries*. While overseas Chinese businessmen may not be keen about doing business with the Communists, they find it difficult to turn down opportunities to make a profit.

No matter what China policy the United States pursues, the entire Orient is likely in the years ahead to be dominated again, as it has been for most of the last two millennia, by its massive heartland neighbor.

The Middle East

It has been my good fortune to visit the Middle East many times. In 1941 I traveled through Turkey, Syria, Iraq, and Iran. In 1952 I visited United States military installations from Morocco to Turkey. In several subsequent trips I traveled in Egypt, Algeria, Morocco, Turkey, Kuwait, Bahrein, Jordan, and Lebanon. But the most interesting and thorough trip was in 1955, when my wife and daughter and I got a Renault Frigate in Paris and drove around the Mediterranean. The East started for us when we were still in Europe, with the magnificence of Granada's Alhambra. Across the ferry in Ceuta, where Francisco Franco began his rebellion, we were in the Arab world. We stayed in it for three months.

As in Asia and most of Latin America, the hunger and poverty were almost universal. In Morocco's Marrakech and Mouley Idris and even in Tangier we saw men living along yard-wide streets and tunnels, filthy, stinking; hungry, scabby children, eyes black with the tenacious flies, begging, screaming, dying. In sharp contrast were the pin-neat United States air bases, with their symmetric installations and clean-cut sun-tanned Aryan personnel. On the other leg of the triangular extreme were Volubilis and the ancient ruins near Tangier of one of Carthage's strongest outposts. Here ancient empires had maintained their garrisons against the barbarians of the day, as we today are doing.

We had a stupid, stilted audience with El Glouie, Pasha of Marrakech, and far more interesting talks with several furtive revolutionaries, whose names I was not told, but whom I was to meet again as cabinet ministers after independence.

In Algeria the revolt was just beginning, so we gaped uneasily at the beauties of the winding coastal road and pushed on into Tunisia. From there, from the massive ruins of ancient Carthage, we drove steadily for nearly a month across the desert.

During this tiring arid trek, along the endless road fought for so bitterly by Rommel and Montgomery, past the sand-swept bones of war—Gabes, Tripoli, Benghazi, Tobruk, Alamein, and into Egypt—the importance of one basic element was driven into our aching sweaty heads: water.

WATER

One can pore over the "Ancient Mariner" or Karl August Wittvegel's hydraulic societies, but a drive across the Libyan desert and indeed along the whole southern coast of the Mediterranean gives one full consciousness of this key regional problem.

Yet this is a problem made by man. For it is human improvidence that turned the fertile fields of antiquity into the deserts of today. Along our road we visited a dozen ancient ruins, some newly dug from the shifting sand, ruins of ancient cities along the coasts of Tunisia, Libya, Egypt, and even further east, cities built by the Romans, some of them on the foundations of even older cities built by the Phoenicians or their misty antecedents. These cities were once ports, from whose wharves ships set sail bearing the grain and olive oil produced in those days on the fertile coastal plain and exported to less fertile lands like Greece and Italy. During those golden days the seasonal rains were retained by the roots of trees in the heavily forested mountains behind the plains. Primitive but effective canals brought the water down to nourish olive grove and vine and field.

But man neglected nature's bounty. Trees were cut down and not replanted. The *coup de grâce* was delivered by the seventh-century Arab invaders, whose goats, sheep, and camels ate the seedlings. Within a century the mountains were bare of trees. Winter rains ran off in flash floods into the Mediterranean, washing away the fertile soil.

In Mesopotamia, the same thing occurred but under different auspices. Here fertility's executioners were the Mongol invaders of the twelfth century, who razed the elaborate irrigation system started five thousand years earlier by the Sumerians, and gradually improved by the Assyrians, Babylonians, Persians, and Kurds. A thousand years ago the population of what we now call Iraq was probably about twenty-five million. Today flying out of Baghdad, I could see the outlines of the ancient canals, but Iraq's five million people are largely hungry.

For lack of water the Middle East has become steadily poorer year by year. Economic crises and political instabilities are tied to the question of water. There is not enough water to irrigate enough land to raise enough food to nourish the population.

So long as this situation prevails it will make little difference what redivisions of wealth are carried out, what land reforms or nationalization of business and industry are suggested. The Arab governments could, and may, nationalize oil as Nasser nationalized the Suez Canal. It would bring spectacular revenue to a few, but it probably would do little to solve the land's basic economic imbalance. Only water can do that.

As we drove eastward, over the abominable roads of western Egypt, over the desert to the incredibly fertile Nile Valley and perenially magnificent Cairo and onward through the Levant, I encountered the Middle East's second regional preoccupation, the Arab-Israeli conflict.

THE ARAB-ISRAELI CONFLICT

Eastward from the huge desert monument at Alamein, which the British erected to fallen friend and foe alike, we heard with ever mounting frequency acrimonious conflicting claims by the Arabs and the Jews that Palestine is *their* land.

Some four thousand years ago numbers of primitive Semitic tribesmen roamed the hills of Palestine, grazing their sheep, fishing, learning agriculture. In about 1600 B.C. a famine scourged the area, and one tribe, led by a man named Joseph, fled to Egypt, where at first it prospered, later was enslaved. For some five centuries this tribe lived among the then cosmopolitan and sophisticated Egyptians, absorbing culture and technology but remaining essentially unassimilated. Finally, led by Moses, the Jews, as they had begun to think of themselves, fled Egypt and after forty years of wandering came again to Palestine. There they found their Semitic cousins, not yet conscious of being Arabs, living the primitive and precarious lives from which the Jews had fled half a millennium earlier. The Jews invaded, triumphed, and settled. And from then on for nearly twenty centuries Palestine was Jewish, though it was governed by a series of conquerors, including the Babylonians, the Hittites, the Syrians, and the Romans.

Then came Mohammed and the great Arab awakening. Fired with Messianic enthusiasm and armed with the faith and sword of the Prophet, the Arabs swarmed over most of the Mediterranean world and in the process made life difficult for the Jews, many of whom fled to Europe. For the next dozen centuries Palestine was an Arab land, though ruled at times by the Crusaders, Turks, the French, and the British. At the turn of the present century the Jews began their return to Palestine. But during the 1920's the then British mandate of Palestine still had a substantial Arab majority. Even in 1949 it would have had an Arab majority had not some million Arabs found themselves,

on the termination of hostilities, separated from their homes by the frontiers of what had become the state of Israel.

Thus, historically, both Jews and Arabs have a case.

But during recent years constant warfare, steady new immigration into Israel, and the mass misery of the Arab refugees, who constitute more than half the population of Jordan and exist precariously on United Nations handouts, have fanned the Arab-Israeli conflicts into a horror which threatens at any time to engulf the Middle East in war.

Aided by public and private subsidies, the diligent Israelis have made the desert bloom and have established both an operative democracy and the highest per capita income in that part of the world. But they have done little to earn the confidence or good will of their Arab neighbors, who outnumber them by nearly fifty to one. Nor did the Israelis improve matters when they invaded Sinai in 1956.

Though at present the Israeli economy is patently inviable without its subsidies, it could capitalize on the energy and skill of its citizens and carve out for itself a place like that of little Holland in medieval Europe—prosperity based on trade, intensive agriculture, and specialized manufacture. But such a position would of necessity depend on friendly relations with the neighboring states. The Arabs on their side could learn much from their traveled cousins.

Driving through the area, through Lebanon, Syria, Jordan, to Turkey, we saw the refugees—thirty-five thousand in one camp in Jericho. We heard their impassioned pleas for justice. We also saw conclusive evidence that Arab leaders from Cairo to Baghdad were bending every effort to prevent any solution of the refugee question, which will have to rest eventually on resettlement, probably in Iraq.

Could both sides be prevailed upon to make concessions? Only, I believe, as a part of a general international Middle Eastern development plan. Without some such development the

Arab-Israeli conflict is bound to fester on, poisoning the whole area and constantly threatening a Korean-type war financed and supplied by the great powers.

OIL

Further eastward, on another trip, I had a chance to study another major regional problem—oil. For Iraq, Iran, Saudi Arabia, and the Persian Gulf sheikdoms among them have more than half the world's now known petroleum reserves. In Iraq, Kuwait, and Bahrein I had a chance to look over fields and refineries, talk with Arab workers, supercilious sheiks in lemon Cadillacs, and dusty laconic British and American drillers and engineers.

Three points came clearly through these talks: first, the oil revenue is now so unevenly distributed between the wealthy few and the destitute many that violent revolution lurks constantly around every Middle Eastern corner. Second, the Western companies, for want of better social patterns, have made their agreements and given the revenue to the bloated few, while through trade schools and grass-roots industrial democracy, sowing seeds bound to ripen into rebellion soon against the recognized regal authorities. This, plus the resentment of those unhappy Middle Eastern states like Lebanon, Syria, and Egypt, who have so far produced no oil, but who act as hosts for pipe lines and canals without which the oil of their luckier neighbors would be worthless, maintain the whole area in a state of explosive instability.

These diverse tensions, along with the crisscrossed great-power conflicts converging on the Middle East, conflicts for oil, warm-water ports, and the control of canals and pipe lines, make the Middle East the powder keg it is. I found some local statesmen able to look beyond the din and dust of battle to some ultimate solutions: Fadhil Jamali, who has since been jailed; Charles Malik, who became engrossed in his duties as President of the United Nations General Assembly; Gamal Abdel Nasser, who is pushed increasingly by forces he does not control.

Africa

Our African trip started in Dakar, with its unique N'Gor Hotel overlooking the Atlantic, its spectacular public buildings, its urbane Negro intelligentsia, all outgrowths of the best of French colonialism. We drove up into Senegal, with a French African official with more university education than I have; and we walked through quaint villages, ports, and marts. In one I noticed a small boy with fingernail-sized amulets on his arm and asked our guide what they were. "They are *gris-gris*," he said. "They protect the boy from evil."

"Do you believe in *gris-gris*?" I asked.

He shrugged. "As an educated man I cannot believe in such superstitions. On the other hand, as a man of sense, I cannot ignore them," he said.

Here was Black Africa in a sentence. One foot in the tribal past, one in the swift-moving twentieth century.

Farther down the coast another African gave me another key sentence. "We do not like the French. We want to be independent, and we will be. But I must admit the French did one useful thing for us—they stopped the tribal wars and introduced a common law."

In Abidjan we gaped at architecture which would have done credit to our biggest state capitals. In Freetown we gaped again at the converse, a city slumbering for a half century without any new construction, a monument to the British policies of making their colonies pay their own way.

Liberia was sobering. Here a country, independent since its birth, had lower indices of education and economic progress than most of its neighbors, British and French colonies.

Nigeria and the Cameroons presented the same comparison. The French were spending money, preparing their colonies for integration into what they hoped would be a huge and happy union under the tricolor. The British were getting ready to leave, preparing for independence as soon as orderly transfers of power could be arranged.

GHANA

Ghana was fascinating. We sat absorbed for two days in the Parliament and listened to both good-natured and acrimonious debate. We talked with smiling, shining ministers and their laconic British parliamentary secretaries. We visited a fishing village, the new port, the site of an immense power and aluminum project which will diversify the currently prosperous but vulnerable one-crop economy. We inspected the new and magnificent university. In many ways Ghana is a test-tube country.

ALBERT SCHWEITZER

In French Equatorial Africa we had two days with Albert Schweitzer in his Forest Hospital, an experience I shall long remember and with mixed feelings.

In an Air France DC-3 we hopped from gravel strip to strip, along with local passengers—sweating women trailing burlap bags, blackened pots, and wide-eyed children, like a rural bus in Mexico. From Douala, Pont Noir, then inland to Lambarene —population, forty Europeans, several thousand Africans— "they come and they go." We disembarked and bounced over a jungle trail in a jeep some two miles to the Oguwe River, where a wiry African, face furrowed with tribal marks, agreed to take us up the muddy river in his pirogue—hollow log canoe—to the hospital for 200 francs each.

After an hour's hard paddling, we reached the rambling complex of low barracks, where a score of European doctors and nurses, headed by the remarkably robust eighty-three-year-old Schweitzer, care for some four hundred Africans, sick with everything from leprosy and yaws to broken legs and infected teeth, and as many relatives of all ages. Patients come from scores of miles through steaming jungle in their pirogues. Sometimes, loath to leave when cured, they stay on as nurses, gardeners, builders. Goats, chickens, naked children, tame gazelles, and a full-grown male chimpanzee recovering from a broken leg swarmed the compound, smoky from tiny fires, where garrulous half-naked women made broth in blackened pots for their sick husbands.

Around the compound we were shown hundreds of fruit trees, planted reverently by Schweitzer over thirty years ago. These, and a beautifully tended garden, supplied much of the food for the European personnel and guests, who eat in a large common dining room presided over by the white-maned, impatient Alsatian patriarch and humanist, who, as he told me, had "spent a lifetime doing what I can to enlighten and humanize our culture."

After dinner, after a sixteenth-century German hymn with Schweitzer at the out-of-tune piano and some Bible passages, read by the doctor in his native German, we were invited to his cluttered study. Here were books, reports, test tubes, sheaves of clippings from the New York *Times,* some bits of fish being carried from the desk by a swarm of ants. (He likes ants—part of his reverence for life, the nurse said.)

The doctor shook his head. "I am but an old man in the forest. Perhaps I should stick to my medicine, to Africa. But how can I now keep silent when I see the mad determination with which man is preparing to destroy himself? The house is burning. The tests must stop. You and the Russians must come to an understanding. . . ."

Then we talked of Africa, and here the doctor demonstrated that his sociology, like his medicine, is somewhat dated. He regarded the Africans essentially as children, with whom one must be fair but firm. Mixing the races at meals or in the wards would not make sense. Yes, political independence was coming to the whole continent, he said, but "political independence without economic independence is meaningless." A pertinent piece of elementary wisdom.

THE MIGHTY CONGO

In the Belgian Congo we took a boat trip, three days downstream from Stanleyville to Coquilhatville, winding among the shifting sandbars and verdant islands on whose shores grinning natives live in grass shacks without windows or doors, pick wild bananas, fish the muddy river, and carry on their age-old game of survival with the crocodiles. They speak languages which have no word for "work." They know neither the plow nor the wheel. This in a valley at least as large and rich as the Mississippi's. Who will persuade or force these simple people to work, to clear the land, and till the soil? Not the Belgians. It is the wrong century. It must be the Congolese themselves.

And in Leopoldville I talked with two young African leaders elected district burgomasters in the Congo's first elections months before. Vigorous and intelligent men they were. They spoke of trouble, perhaps as soon as five years hence, if the Belgians dragged their feet on self-government. Later, Belgian officials told me, frowning, that trouble might indeed occur in ten years. Actually, within six months dozens were killed in widespread rioting, and my two African leaders found themselves in jail.

We went on south, to the Union of South Africa and from the Union, after a few days in the relaxed air of Portugal's huge "province," Mozambique, to Salisbury, the throbbing capital of the Central African Federation. An afternoon at home with fabulous, 300-pound Prime Minister Sir Roy Welensky, onetime professional boxer, locomotive engineer, and union leader, produced some answers; and others came during a visit to the copper belt for an on-the-spot inspection of one of the richest and most productive industries of the rich continent. Less harassed than the Union by racial tensions, the Rhodesias face the same dilemma.

A week in Tanganyika and a short visit to fabled Zanzibar, producer of most of the world's cloves, started us up through

East Africa. In Nairobi we learned that the Kikuyus' Mau Mau insurrection, though crushed, had, in fact, won, in that the country's white settlers have, for the most part, reconciled themselves to an African-governed Kenya within a decade. Here I had a talk with one of Africa's most impressive young leaders, twenty-nine-year-old Tom Mboya, who knows more about the continent's basic problems than anyone I had seen.

A sweltering stay in the Sudan en route made us appreciate the cool eight-thousand-foot freshness of Addis Ababa. Never had I been so conscious of the benefits of colonialism than in this backward land, independent since the legendary days of King Solomon. Visiting the university and the impressive Russian hospital, I began formulating my questions and answers on Africa and groping for their meaning. I worked at the task during a week in Egypt, and then on to Europe.

WHY SO BACKWARD?

Its oppressive poverty aside, Africa's principal problems seemed to be its backwardness and its heterogeneity.

Considering the developmental job to be done in Africa, I asked: Why is the Dark Continent so backward? Why has progress been so halting, retrogression so frequent?

In the Transvaal remains have been found of a collateral cousin of ours, *Australopithecus prometheus,* who long before the last glacial age learned simple speech and the use of fire, then disappeared. Cave paintings in South Africa give glimpses of a vigorous hunting and fishing society in that area many thousands of years ago. But when Europeans first came to South Africa in the fifteenth century, they found it empty, save for a handful of miserable Bushmen, who had retreated southward before the massive Bantu *völkerwanderung.*

The Arabs, Chinese, and also the ancient Persians landed in Madagascar and East Africa some two thousand years ago, but they never penetrated the interior and had such trouble with disease that they limited their activities to some trading and slaving and then often withdrew of their own accord from what even then seems to have been a forbidding continent.

For several thousand years a series of great Mediterranean cultures traded along the coasts, built fortresses against inland barbarians, fought each other. Along with other unknown contemporaries in Mesopotamia, India, and distant China, they invented tools, wrote books, constructed philosophies, composed plays and poems. Why did the Africans remain until but yesterday contentedly static, backward savages?

Several answers spring to mind. The heat, the desert, the tsetse fly, and always, "our best young men and women were enslaved." Yet India's climate is as hot and unhealthy; Arabia and China have their deserts; and as for slavery, why were not the Africans making slaves of the Arabs and the Portuguese?

Racist theorists snort that the blacks are obviously inferior and document their claims with Biblical quotations, psuedo-scientific tests.

None of these answers is adequate. And I found in going through my notes that my perplexity was shared by many able Africans like Tom Mboya, who had told me, "If I did not have some other things to do, I should like to return to Cambridge and try a doctoral thesis on the reasons for our backwardness."

True, some suggested that more skillful archeologists and anthropologists may uncover African achievements still unknown and demonstrate that the continent's history is not so much poor as poorly known.

But I was forced to leave the question as currently unanswerable and move on to sort out the varied expressions of this historic backwardness.

FRAGMENTED CONTINENT

One day in Nigeria's capital, Lagos, an African functionary learned that Mrs. Scott was Russian. "Russian?" he said in fascination. "Do the Russians have a common language?" This preoccupation is a reflection of the fact that 220 million Africans speak at least 600 distinct languages, only three or four of which had achieved their own script prior to the coming of the white man. Most Africans can speak to each other only in English or French or Arabic. In a city like Lagos, language barriers are frequently crossed when crossing a street.

Even in individual countries like Kenya or Nigeria or Ghana, no single African language is generally spoken, and the decision reached recently in Accra to make English the official language of Ghana reflects a general realization in Africa that no African language can meet the demands of the Africans for a national language to go with the shiny new or soon-to-be national independence.

True, East Africa has a lingua franca in Swahili, that strange linguistic hybrid, invented a thousand years ago by Arab slavers out of bits and pieces of a dozen tongues. But if Swahili is easy to learn, it is also limited in vocabulary and expressiveness, and most local Africans like Tom Mboya have definitely rejected it in favor of English as the official language of the future.

In Tunisia and Morocco the same position was recently recognized by the respective ministries of education, which officially adopted French rather than Arabic as the language of instruction in higher schools because of paucity of teachers and textbooks in Arabic.

Associated with the language problem is the issue of future federations.

The recent declaration by Ghana and Guinea has pinpointed a tendency for young African states to associate themselves into some kind of organization in order better to negotiate with huge foreign units of power like the Common Market, and to plan and co-ordinate economies which must to some degree be interdependent.

In my travels I found the outlines shaping up for several large regional federations:

1. A North African Federation, already called *Maghreb*—Arabic for "the West"—including Morocco, Tunisia, and Al-

geria; population, about twenty-five million; languages, French and Arabic.

2. A West African Federation, consisting of present French West Africa plus Gambia, Sierra Leone, Ghana, Liberia, Nigeria, and Togoland; population, about sixty million; languages, English and French.

3. A Congo Federation, including the Belgian Congo, French Equatorial Africa, Ruanda-Urundi, and perhaps the Cameroons; language, French; population, twenty million.

4. An East African Federation, consisting of Tanganyika, Kenya, Uganda, and perhaps Somalia and the Somalilands; language, English; population, about twenty-two million.

5. A Southern Continental Federation, already urged by many leaders in the Union of South Africa, to include the Union, the Rhodesias and perhaps Nyasaland; languages, English and Afrikaans, at least in the beginning; population, some eighteen million.

The place in this possible future political evolution of Egypt, Madagascar, Ethiopia, and the Portuguese colonies is questionable. But the federations I have outlined above make elementary linguistic, economic, and administrative sense; and I found them being seriously discussed by thoughtful Africans and Europeans right across the continent.

THE CANCER OF RACISM

A final problem faced more acutely by Africa than by other areas of the Hungry World is racism.

For in the Union, the Rhodesias, and in another form in Algeria, racial discrimination, interwoven with the economic issues arising from foreign land ownership, has engulfed thirty million human beings in a conflict which bids fair to poison the atmosphere of the entire continent.

My conviction that white land tenure constitutes a central element in this issue is based on the fact that in Black Africa, where the whites are few and own no land, race relations are amicable.

Summary

Through all Africa and most of Latin America and Asia I found this to be true: people were poor and getting poorer. Most of the world's children are undernourished, poorly clothed, inadequately housed. For millions, shoes and schools are luxuries quite beyond reach or expectation.

The Hungry World finds itself caught in the trap of its own fertility and the economics of residual colonialism, writhing in misery, watching the developed countries get steadily richer while the underdeveloped get poorer.

It has been known for some time that there was an insidious cycle of causality at work with poverty and disease. The poor man is undernourished and contracts tuberculosis, loses his job, and becomes even poorer, and so forth. This law worked with classical simplicity in the concentration camps of Stalin's Russia, whose survivors describe the blood-chilling inevitability which pursued the prisoner who allowed his production to fall below the norm for even one day. His food ration was cut. The following day he was weaker, and his production fell even more. So did his ration, and so on in progression to the end. Aware of this, prisoners strained with might and main to avoid falling below the norm even for one day. And this, indeed, was the intention of the authorities in instituting the system.

And this cycle is at work today on a world-wide scale, without anyone's having planned or willed it. Most Black Africans today, for lack of protein, are lethargic. The lower their productivity falls, the less can they afford to buy, or the less are they able to catch or trap the protein they need.

As Gunnar Myrdal points out in his excellent *Rich Lands and Poor*, "Nothing fails like failure." The Hungry World today faces self-reproducing failure, misery, and poverty, though its citizens often become well informed enough to know about and envy angrily the unused surpluses of the developed countries.

The United Nations Economic Committee for Latin America has analyzed most lucidly the specific implications of this awful process in Latin America, whose nations trade primary goods for industrial goods and services from industrial areas. As per capita income rises above a certain point, the demand for primary products grows less rapidly than that for industrial goods and services. Thus given the same rate of per capita income growth, the demand for industrial imports in underdeveloped countries grows more rapidly than the demand for primary imports in the industrial center. If, in addition, the population of the peripheral area increases more rapidly than that of the center, the disparity is aggravated; and if the per capita income of the periphery increases more rapidly than that of the center, then the imbalance becomes even more marked. As an added misfortune to the underdeveloped countries, the industrial nations keep developing new synthetic products to replace their imports of primary goods—nylon for silk, synthetic quinine and rubber.

Aware of this awful cycle, philanthropists and men of good will have sought to allay its consequences by giving medicines and food, clothing, and building materials to the Hungry World. Alas, the results were often the opposite of those intended. The child whose life was saved by silver nitrate or a CARE package has, within two decades, begotten several children whose prospects of becoming self-sufficient under the existing economy are smaller than were his.

Other conscionable representatives of the developed countries have held that political and economic democracy could release productive forces like those that developed the developed countries of today. They forget perhaps that the race has quadrupled since the Napoleonic Wars, and human demands and expectations have also increased.

Neither democracy nor philanthropy is enough. To break this

cursed cycle it is clear that economic development is mandatory. The citizens of the Hungry World must be made capable of feeding themselves.

The capital, equipment, and the know-how to do this job are what the United States has to offer the world.

Three ⚭ Trials and Errors

Through all the Hungry World I saw nationalists of varied sizes and stripes coping, nearly always in the name of the "people," with similar problems: the winning of independence and the running of their countries.

Having recorded visual and oral impressions of some sixty nations of the Hungry World, I now have chosen, for more detailed treatment, eight typical of success or failure in different phases of their complex task. I have picked those which seemed to have the most direct implications for our attitudes and our policies.

Bolivia: Turning Success into Failure

Bolivia achieved its independence more than a century ago, in 1826. Landlocked and remote in their mountains, chances seemed good that the sturdy, llama-herding inhabitants of the altiplano could organize and run their country satisfactorily. But, alas, they became involved in one of the ninetecnth-century's three most destructive conflicts, the Chaco War*—which killed almost a third of the Bolivian people.

---

* The others: China's T'aip'ing Rebellion and the American Civil War. All three were far more destructive than the relatively humane Napoleonic Wars.

Then came the development of the country's fabulous tin deposits. European banks put up the capital, and local strong men like Simon Patiño ran the enterprises. Tin was produced in large quantities; millions were made by the banks and a few local industrialists; tens of thousands of Bolivian miners labored long for little, longed for better days, and died of silicosis.

In 1952 Bolivia underwent a revolution. The tin miners organized an army, defeated the forces of the government, nationalized the mines, and proceeded to run the country. But they did so without due regard for economic fundamentals. They passed labor legislation, doubtless long overdue, instituted special reduced-price commissaries for the miners; and, fed up with generations of exploitation, eased in their work to the point where an average miner at the face worked only three hours a day—and thousands, comfortably featherbedded above ground, did no productive work.

All this increased the production costs of Bolivian tin to a point some 20 per cent above its world market price. The difficulties were in part caused by the companies, who, anticipating the nationalization, had withdrawn working capital, and allowed the equipment inventory to fall below standards. But the fact was that the Bolivian economy had become inviable.

Into this nasty economic void the United States stepped, with subsidies which ran to some twenty-five million dollars annually during the past six years. That this could not continue indefinitely was obvious to any intelligent Bolivian. Either the miners would have to mine tin more cheaply, or move down into the valleys and take up farming.

When I visited the country, American aid authorities were organizing development projects in the valleys, in a desperate attempt to reorientate the country's bankrupt economy. But the Bolivians did not like the valleys. They could not breathe there properly, they said; and indeed tuberculosis was a problem among those who did undertake the change.

When I asked Bolivians what they saw ahead, they usually

shrugged. Inflation was already out of control, and it was clear that the United States would soon get tired of the aid program. "Perhaps it was all a mistake," I heard several Bolivians remark. "Perhaps we should not have become a nation."

It was unfortunate that in 1959 violence was touched off by a similar remark attributed to an American diplomat. The reaction, like so much else in Bolivia, was childish. Like a man with a fever smashing the thermometer against the wall and cursing the doctor, the Bolivians who stoned the United States Embassy were demonstrating the failure of Bolivia, after five generations, to govern itself.

For the past three years, tough President Hernán Siles Zuazo has been striving to infuse into these rugged mountain people a sense of realism and discipline. His program has been sound: raise taxes, raise labor productivity, stop printing money, reduce the preposterous above-ground mining bureaucracy, cut the commissary subsidies. He has had help from the International Monetary Fund as well as the United States. But his achievements have been negligible. Neither the party bureaucrats nor the miners seem willing to try to balance production with consumption.

Perhaps the fact that only 2.8 per cent of Bolivia's children are in school is a partial explanation for the country's lack of discipline. In any case, at this writing, the IMF is holding up further payments pending some indications from La Paz that Siles's program is being implemented.

In the meantime, one can only regret that both independence and self-government seem to have failed in Bolivia.

South Africa: Terminal Cancer?

The Union of South Africa has been independent for nearly three generations; and, unlike Bolivia, has been most successful in organizing the economy of that bounteous country. And a bounteous country indeed it is, with its fine climate and fabulous mineral and agricultural wealth. The Union of South Africa was not just discovered—it was built, by some three million European South Africans and their doughty ancestors. But, in the process, they used the labor and sometimes the lands of the Bushmen and Hottentots, the recently arrived Bantus, the million or so "colored" progeny of forbidden miscegenation, and nearly half a million Indians brought in as indentured labor to work the sugar plantations of Natal.

These ten million luckless men and women, disenfranchised, humiliated, de-tribalized, still largely uncivilized, are held in virtual economic serfdom for the benefit of the "master"—as I constantly heard myself being called. With sullen natives pushing the crime rate to a world record in these fragmented and segregated communities, the beauty and bounty of this land is embittered in shame and fear, badly concealed by arrogance and bigotry.

At Kimberley, I saw diamonds being mined. The skilled work, planning, and supervision were done by some 300 Europeans; the drilling, digging, clearing, and "helping" by some two thousand "boys" (as the white men call natives of any age) who come from far and wide on contracts, which average less than a year. They are housed in two tidy, hygienic compounds, from which the miners go down directly for their forty-eight-hour week of labor in the mines. To prevent theft of the gems, the men are confined for the duration of their contracts to the hostel and mine, though on week ends they may talk through a grill to wives and relatives who come to visit from their tribal native "reserves." The average take-home pay is about ten dollars per month.

Capetown, one of the Union's two federal capitals, is the New Orleans of South Africa: beautiful, relaxed, cosmopolitan, and liberal—by South African standards. In its two universities, several score of dark-skinned students share the same classrooms with their European fellow countrymen. In rush hours, black and white even ride the same streetcars. But the city's primary school system is segregated six ways: European (English language); European (Afrikaans language); colored, Indian, Malay, and native. The natives study, during the first three grades, in half a dozen tribal languages, then edge over into English or Afrikaans. As elsewhere in the Union, non-Europeans are restricted to distant and inferior "townships," are paid far less than the whites, and are humiliated in a dozen ways.

Though the Union is far and away the most prosperous nation in Africa, though the climate is ideal and the country still underpopulated, most educated South Africans are almost neurotically preoccupied with "the native question."

During talks with leaders of the Nationalist government and the United party opposition, I learned that nearly all South Africa's three million Europeans agree that they must maintain "control," *i.e.*, keep the natives, colored, Indians, and Malays disenfranchised and restricted as to place of residence, property ownership, occupation, educational opportunity, and freedom of movement. But they clash bitterly over whether *apartheid* should lead eventually to separate Bantu states, whether the pass laws should be vigorously enforced, whether white immigration should be discouraged, whether the Bantus should be restricted to an education designed to prepare them for a position of permanent economic servitude.

The stalwart Boers tend to back the Nationalist government in replying "yes" to all these questions, and are quite prepared to deal with any native "trouble" with machine guns. Other South Africans, including most of the English-speaking 45 per cent of the white community, oppressed with fear and shame and indecision, nevertheless battle this attitude constantly.

A prominent Dutch Reform Church official admitted soberly: "The repressive aspects of *apartheid* cannot be reconciled with Christian teaching." A conservative editor said: "The natives have lost hope, and this leads to crime and rebellion." A top businessman shook his head: "This cannot last. We're just hanging on."

And the best outside opinion I could find holds that the point-of-no-return in South African race relations has been passed—and that violence is inevitable.

Among the surprises I found in the Union was the existence of a fairly large and articulate extreme Left. Though the Communist party is illegal, there are probably some three thousand current card-carriers who work largely through legal fronts: the African National Congress (mostly native); the Congress of Democrats (European); the Congress of Colored People's Organizations; and the South African Indian Congress. These groups hold meetings, raise money, and organize legal defense against relocation, segregation, economic inequities, and government attempts at suppression.

Encouraged by English and some native language broadcasts from Moscow and Cairo, these Communist-led leftists work with diligence, dedication, idealism, and interracial comradeship against *apartheid*. Leadership is mostly white and, as in similar groups in Europe, often Jewish; but influence among natives is growing. One important result soon to come, I think, will be native trade unions, for whose development every legitimate prerequisite exists, though so far the government has outlawed and crushed every budding local.

Distressingly, I found virtually no attempt being made in South Africa to wrest leadership of this legitimate leftist movement from the Communists. Both major parties are conservative, support *apartheid* in principle, and back the heavy-handed enforcement of the Suppression of Communism Law by towering, self-righteous Justice Minister Charles Swart and his open preparations to meet "trouble" with ruthless military repression.

The most reliable observers I encountered predicted ten years or so of continued, tortured tension before a crisis occurs in the Union of South Africa. And what then?

Historically, multiracial societies have dealt with their problems either by the destruction or the expulsion of one racial group by another, or by general amalgamation. White South

Africans cannot adopt the first alternative, because they need the 400,000 native miners and other non-European labor. They refuse fanatically any suggestion of the second. Thus, I am afraid it is now too late to solve the Union's racial problems without violence—violence in which the Europeans may eventually face destruction or expulsion at the hands of the African majority. Meantime, the fires of fear, hatred, and bigotry feed on one another.

Algeria: Bitter War of Independence

Racism and European land ownership and privilege have led to troubles not only in South Africa, but also at the opposite end of the continent. During three visits to Algeria in the past five years, I saw the development of one of this century's most cruel, protracted, and unnecessary wars. For five years, the bitterest kind of fighting has been going on between half a million French troops and a well-organized nationalist guerrilla army under the command of the *Front de Libération Nationale* (FLN).

When the revolt first broke out on November 1, 1954, it was led by a group of nationalist activists, who, dissatisfied with the failure of their politicians to achieve independence for Algeria, organized a concerted terrorist campaign.

In the early months of the rebellion, the nationalist partisans operated in small groups, burning French farms, throwing bombs into cafés, raiding police stations and military posts and convoys for weapons, and engaging in calculated terrorism against those Algerians who collaborated with the French. While a few French settlers did sell out and leave Algeria as unrest spread, departures were limited, mainly because property buyers were hard to find. Most of the *colons* stayed on stubbornly, determined that Algeria would remain French at all costs.

As the cruel war dragged on, the Liberation Army became larger and more professional. By late 1958, it included some

600,000 troops in uniform, operating in organized units under six separate commands and a supreme command, the latter located partly in Tunisia, partly in Algeria, partly in Egypt.

The Liberation troops are paid regular wages, and their families receive allowances. They have a well-organized supply system which brings in arms, munitions, and other matériel by land, sea, and air. They operate hospitals and rehabilitation centers in Tunisia and Morocco, and small combat hospitals in Algeria itself. In whole areas of Algeria, they collect taxes, by both pressure and persuasion, from the French as well as the Moslems. In metropolitan France, they have an effective organization among the 300,000 Algerian workers, from whom taxes are likewise collected. Finally, they are said to have an air force in training, although it is not clear where they will base their planes, or where these planes will be obtained.

All these activities are carried out under the direction of a provisional government located in Cairo, though many of its functionaries despise the Egyptians.

The French, meanwhile, brought to Algeria from NATO's center line five full divisions, together with all their American equipment; and, through various devices, such as the postponement of interest payments, got the United States to carry part of the heavy financial burden of the war. Thus, to most of the Arab world and Africa, it appears that it is not just France who is fighting in Algeria—but America, too.

But if military victory is not in sight for the French, neither is it for the FLN. When I inquired of leaders on both sides as to their prospects, their answers where surprisingly similar. "We will go on fighting," they said, in effect, "because we cannot stop."

In France, as the cost and casualties of the Algerian war mounted, politicians defending the policy of "pacification of the rebels" persuaded the French public that the oil in the Sahara would be the panacea for all the woes of France in Algeria.

Oil was discovered in the Algerian Sahara near the Libyan

frontier shortly after World War II. By 1956, even conservative oil experts became convinced that the reserves amounted to some half a billion barrels. At this point, Saharan oil became a major political issue: "Algeria must remain French for the sake of Saharan oil, if nothing else!" Frenchmen were made to feel that this future oil wealth made it "impossible" for France to give in to nationalist demands for independence.

However, despite colonial pride and the dream of oil, a great deal of critical thinking has recently been going on in France about the economics of Algeria in peace and in war. The estimates indicate that currently the French are spending about $1.3 billion a year for military operations in Algeria, or about 20 per cent of France's national budget.

A recent confidential report, circulated in France by government economists critical of the pursuance of the Algerian war, points out that unless France is willing and able to meet the economic challenges of Algeria after a successful conclusion to the war, the war itself loses all moral justification. Yet the expense necessary to secure an appreciable rise in living standards among the Moslem population of Algeria would be truly enormous. With its population increase coefficient at about 2.6 per cent, Algeria's population in 1980 can be expected to constitute eighteen million Moslems and 1.25 million Europeans. The cost of sending Algerian children to school would be about $500 million a year. The annual capital expenditure necessary to increase Algerian annual per capita income by 2 per cent a year—assuming that the Algerian war were suddenly and happily terminated tomorrow, without the loss of any further lives or property—amounts to $250 million annually now, increasing to $950 million per year by 1980.

Charles de Gaulle faced these realities squarely in his historic speech in Constantine in October 1958, where he outlined a program of partial industrialization for Algeria, and an equalization in the educational opportunities and living standards of the

Algerians with those in metropolitan France. The ten-year program would cost France a staggering four billion dollars in the
first five years alone.

Certain French economists and businessmen, aware of these
facts, have come to the conclusion that even if the Algerian war
could be won immediately it is doubtful whether France could
afford the luxury of economic association with, and responsibility for, Algeria.

Of course, the gravity of Algeria's economic problems would
not be diminished if the country were to win independence. But
the Algerians rather than the French would have to worry about
that. In all events, it would be much easier for an independent
Algerian government to persuade the population to accept continued low living standards than for the French to do so while
claiming that Algerians and Frenchmen had equal rights and
privileges.

Does the FLN represent the Algerian people? Would it give
the country democratic government? By answering "No" to both
these questions, the French justify their refusal to negotiate with
the representatives of the provisional government on anything
but a cease-fire. It is my impression that most Algerians want
independence, which they would immediately merge into a
federation with neighbors, Morocco and Tunisia. This is what
the FLN is fighting for, often using brutal measures against
deserters and collaborators.

As to the prospects for democratic government under the
FLN after independence, I would guess that its realization will
require at least a decade.

And so the Algerian war goes on, although the French cannot
afford to fight it—or even win it—and cannot hope to achieve,
in any case, what the ignorant want: a perpetuation of colonialism. On the other hand, I feel that Algerian nationalism is
almost sure to win. Why, then, continue fighting? Principally
because the French so far seem unable to face these realities.

Morocco: Limited Success

Directly affected by the Algerian war is the Kingdom of Morocco, with its eight million Berber and Arab subjects, and its still prominent French minority of some 250,000.

While the Algerians and others have paid and are still paying a heavy price for their independence, the Moroccans got theirs almost free. Because of outside influences—including Dienbienphu, the Algerian war, and diplomatic pressure from the United States—the French gave way almost gracefully on March 2, 1956. Morocco became an independent state long before its most ardent nationalists had dreamed it possible—and long before they were actually prepared to run the country.

When I revisited Morocco in September 1958, I found that the nationalist leaders, whom I had seen earlier in exile or in hiding, had become ministers and other high government officials running a constitutional monarchy without a constitution! Substantial numbers of French, Spanish, and American troops still occupied bases in Morocco; the Algerian war was blazing along the borders, while at home neolithic tribesmen and caids stood face to face with a left-wing urban proletariat and a confused French-educated intelligentsia.

There was a good deal of talk about democracy. Everyone, from the King to leftist trade-union leaders, repeatedly proclaimed that Morocco must move toward the Democratic Ideal —but, in practice, no elections had been held; no opposition party was functioning effectively; and government consisted of an endless series of *ad hoc* compromises. Even limited democracy seemed to be still a dozen years off; and the more immediate job appeared to be the reorganization of the administration on a communal rather than a tribal basis.

In the meantime, King Mohammed V, descendant of the Prophet Mohammed, religious and secular sovereign of Morocco, rules with a strong and flexible hand. Unlike Iraq's unfortunate monarch, who counted on conservative leadership to develop his country, Morocco's King called on left-wing political leaders to govern when the Right proved ineffectual.

While some of Morocco's politicians are intensely republican, and believe that monarchies have lived their day, all agree that, as a popular symbol of unity, the forty-nine-year-old autocrat is a major asset to his country, well worth the expenses of his court and the occasional embarrassment caused by his numerous family.

However, plans are being made for Morocco's political future. Suave, cautious Ahmed Balafrej, fifty, then Prime Minister of his country, gave me a blueprint:

It is obvious, for the moment, that the Moroccan voter is not prepared to make wise political judgments on current issues. The uneducated Moroccan is an easy prey for demagogy. For the present, there is no effective opposition here; but we can reach both our economic goals and work toward parliamentary democracy within ten or fifteen years in these steps:

1. Communal elections in late 1959 or 1960.

2. A consultative legislature indirectly elected by the communal councils in 1961 or 1962.

3. A written constitution by 1963. This might be drawn up either by a constitutional committee, duly authorized by the consultative legislature, or by a special constituent assembly elected by special elections. The constitution when written should be widely publicized, discussed, duly changed, and improved, and finally presented to the King for acceptance.

4. A legislative assembly elected as provided for by the constitution should, with the King, work out the problems of an operative constitutional democratic monarchy. During this stage, an effective opposition should appear, and enjoy freedom of expression in presenting its platform and program to the public. This should be accomplished by 1968.

Here was a leader who recognized that democracy would not work at the present time in his country, but who had a fairly clear idea of how to move in the right direction.

In his comfortably cluttered office, graying, trim Deputy Prime Minister and Minister of National Economy, Abderrahim Bouabid, thirty-eight, reflected similar preoccupation with the educational and, above all, economic development of his country as a necessary prerequisite of democracy. He emphasized the necessity to increase production and push for higher investments as a steppingstone to democracy.

Bouabid reviewed for me some of independent Morocco's efforts to spur economic development:

In an attempt to increase investments from the private sector abroad, the Moroccan government passed an investment law in 1958, guaranteeing the convertibility of profits and repatriation of investments according to schedules to be worked out in individual contracts between investors and the Moroccan government. Since independence, several important investors have signed agreements to start operations in Morocco—among them General Tire & Rubber, Simca-Fiat, Volvo, and ENI (the Italian state oil company).

One of the main sources of Moroccan governmental income is the state phosphate monopoly. Last year, Bouabid upset some of his colleagues by allocating the entire eight-billion-francs revenue from this source to investment, thus leaving a gaping fissure in the operational budget. His remedy: cut the cost of operations. Accordingly, the defense and security budget was cut by one-sixth, and the King's salary was cut by about 3 per cent. It was obvious, however, that these measures were not sufficient. "Morocco must have a modern taxation system," Bouabid told me. "At the present time, there is virtually no personal income tax, while corporate taxes are extremely low [20 per cent average]." While regretting that no personal income tax was enforced or in prospect, Bouabid commented with candor: "Before we can collect income tax, we have to get incomes up high enough to be worth taxing."

The Moroccan economy is and for sometime must remain predominantly agricultural—46 per cent of the GNP comes from farming, while 80 per cent of the population lives by agriculture. Moroccan agriculture has been plagued by the concentration of enormous tracts of the best lands in the hands of the French settlers—while side by side with these good farms, the minute, Moroccan-owned farms struggle desperately and inefficiently for survival. To deal with this problem, the Moroccan government originated Operation Tractor in 1957. This involves bringing hundreds of tractors into Morocco, many of them on long-term credit from United States firms, and other mechanized equipment to cultivate co-operatively the inefficient small farms. To popularize the operation, the King himself got out on a tractor in each of several farm centers. As a result, many small farmers agreed to pool their plots of land for large-scale co-operative ploughing and sowing, though they continued to own them individually.

Though the French in 1955 were talking darkly of being pushed into the sea by Islamic hordes if the French government agreed to independence for Morocco, actually nothing, of the kind occurred. Nearly all the French remained, and there has been no record of fatal violence against a Frenchman since independence. The French have remained in control of numerous large farms, and of important industries like the lead mines near Oujda. They complain, of course, of having to pay taxes, and that the wages of their Moroccan help have gone up. But they are still doing very well, a fact which Algeria's million Europeans conveniently refuse to see.

Egypt: Success without Democracy

Egypt is rapidly becoming one of the most important countries in Afro-Asia. Since its revolution in 1952, the country has undergone an impressive political renaissance and today has an economy far stronger than it has had for centuries. Industry is working at capacity; investments are up; the decade-long fall in per capita income has been reversed; price and import controls have curtailed inflation; and large quantities of military equipment have been purchased and deployed. The Egyptians have even built a steel mill. These achievements have been used by the government to exert increasing influence over North and East Africa and the Middle East.

Egypt was declared a democratic Arab republic in 1953 and since 1954 has been under the leadership of Gamal Abdel Nasser, elected to the office of President on June 24, 1956, by a majority of 99.9 per cent. The country's constitution guarantees all Egyptians equality before the law, regardless of race, origin, language, or faith. Voting is compulsory* for both men and women over the age of eighteen. Legislative authority is vested in the National Assembly, and the President of the republic is both chief of state and head of the executive branch. Thus, like the Soviet Union, Egypt's constitution is relatively modern and liberal; but, as in the Soviet Union, its implementation is another matter again. Currently, there is but one political party—Nasser's National Union. There is no freedom of the press, speech, or assembly for any dissenting group. Among those denied political freedom is the Communist party, which is thought to have from four to five thousand members, about half of whom are in jail.

Until recently, Egypt's land tenure system was feudal—twelve thousand large landowners owned 34 per cent of the total arable land. A land reform law passed in 1952 limited ownership to 200 acres. All land above this limit was taken by the government for redistribution over a period of five years. A compensation was paid to the landlord equivalent to ten times the annual rental. This program has now been completed, and 62 per cent of Egypt's population who work the land have more of a stake in their country than ever before.

Cotton accounts for about 80 per cent of Egypt's exports. During the past three years Britain has been replaced by the

* Reminiscent of the quip applied to Nazi Germany: "Everything not forbidden is compulsory."

Soviet bloc as the principal buyer of Egyptian cotton. In addition to commercial purchases, the Soviet bloc is currently taking 10 to 15 per cent of Egypt's cotton crop annually, in payment for the $300 million or so in military equipment Egypt has received from Russia and Czechoslovakia.

The Suez Canal brings in a revenue of about $100 million a year. Recently Cairo has let some sixteen million dollars' worth of contracts to three American corporations for deepening and widening the canal so that it can accommodate the large tankers operating between the Middle East and Europe.

During the past two years, the Egyptian government has enforced rigid price controls on necessities, while restricting the importation of luxury goods. The result has been a fairly constant cost of living for the urban masses but a drastic reduction of living standards for the upper classes, whom Nasser considers potentially hostile anyhow. The income from this policy has permitted the government to carry out its ambitious investment plans.

One of Egypt's most spectacular investments is the Helwan steel mill, about twenty miles south of Cairo, on the right bank of the Nile. I spent a day at the mill, which was constructed by the West German firm, DEMAG, at a cost of about thirty-eight million dollars, and which went into operation at the end of July 1958. The plant is run by a staff of about 280 engineers and technicians, of whom eighty are Germans and 200 Egyptians trained in Germany. The basic labor, of course, is Egyptian— paid about forty cents per day.

The Helwan mill is an economic monstrosity or, more exactly, an economic pyramid. There being no coal in Egypt, coke is imported from Germany, the United States, and the Soviet Union, and brought up the river on barges directly to the mill. The iron ore comes from Aswan—600 miles away, over a bad railroad— and is about 45 per cent red hematite, containing no sulphur but quite a bit of phosphorus. Most serious, the Egyptian market cannot absorb the 600,000 tons of steel the mill will produce.

But as a political symbol, the mill is a great success. On the day it went into operation, an impressive ceremony took place, attended by Nasser, the German Ambassador, and other dignitaries. When the first plate went through the plate mill, several hundred Egyptian workers started a snake dance around the equipment. In the course of the dance, one young worker, swept away with emotion, jumped on the hot plate, where he lay sizzling. Two other workers leapt on it and pulled him off. The rescuers lost their feet; the first man was fried.

Here was ritual sacrifice on the altar of the symbol of the twentieth century, the symbol of industry and autarchy, within a stone's throw of those other temples on whose altars other generations of Egyptians made their ritual sacrifices, with perhaps no less enthusiasm, to the symbols of other millennia.

Of course, it will take some time to translate their current enthusiasm into substantial increases in productivity; and it will be even longer before the Helwan steel mill becomes an economically sound proposition. But as a symbol of industrialization and independence, the mill is of major importance both to Egypt and to the Hungry World.

The Egyptian government has received considerable outside aid. West Germany has given a credit of nearly $100 million to Egypt for the purchase of industrial goods in West Germany. The Soviet Union has advanced nearly half a billion dollars in loans and grants.

This does not mean that Nasser has been bought. It would be a mistake indeed to assume that Nasser has become a Soviet puppet. Nasser thinks he is using the Russians, who hope to use him. History will show who gets the best of the bargain. The increased Soviet infiltration in Iraq may well push Egypt back into the Western camp. Nasser, like Tito, seems inclined to such flexible political seesawing. But he is behaving with considerable dignity. His personal honesty is above question, and he does not seem to have been tempted by the kind of corruption to which Middle Eastern leaders frequently succumb. He has given Egypt the best government it has had for many generations. For all his dictatorial leanings, Nasser has become an important symbol of successful authoritarian nationalism and progress, not only for Arab states but also for countries in non-Arab Africa.

If Nasser should vanish from the scene, the situation in Egypt and the Middle East would not improve. On the contrary, an end to Nasser's enlightened dictatorship would probably result in the kind of vulnerable anarchy that is leading Iraq toward a communist rather than a democratic regime.

Indonesia: Guided Democracy

The huge Presidential Palace in Jakarta was ablaze with light, as 600 good-natured Indonesians gathered in the main hall to hear President Sukarno speak. And speak he did—for an hour and twenty minutes—in imagery so simple and with gestures so eloquent that I could understand whole passages without knowing a word of Bahasa. He talked about Indonesia, a new nation, and its meaning; he spoke of the Indonesian Revolution and *merdeka*—freedom.

It was inspiring to watch this vital President, with his masterful showmanship, speaking to a group of his adoring people. But after the speech, after the still painfully Dutch-sounding brass band played the national anthem, the lights were dimmed, and the audience went out into the darker reality of Indonesia: the filthy, overcrowded city, poverty and misery, the stifling bureaucracy, the pervading illiteracy, and the unreality of Indonesia as a nation.

Indonesia is a dispersed, amorphous country, probably less prepared for nationhood than any of its neighbors. The traditional agriculture of the islands is incapable of feeding the present population, let alone the two million or so annual increase; and were it not for emergency aid from the United States, millions of Indonesians would actually starve.

Independent Indonesia must improve its agriculture. It must

have fertilizers, improved seeds, crop rotation. It must have better transportation and refrigeration facilities. New lands must be cleared and plowed, industries built. These things are not just desirable; they are mandatory—but they require capital and hard work.

The Indonesians have no capital and have already borrowed up to the hilt. Worse, they are obsessed with the outdated concept of "exploitation" by foreign capital, and are not inclined to create a climate in which foreign capital will invest in Indonesia.

Still worse, the people are not working effectively. They have legislated themselves a universal forty-hour week, with thirty-five hours for some categories of office workers. They have not grasped the fundamental relationship between production and consumption. "Now we are free, why should we work?" I heard many say again and again. Sukarno's Huey-Long-type speeches, in effect, encourage this delusion and the resulting imbalance.

Some Indonesians are aware of the need for austerity and effort. Prime Minister Djuanda told me that in 1956 Indonesia's gross national product increased by 1.3 per cent, while the population went up by 1.6 per cent. While Sukarno makes speeches, Djuanda, an engineer by profession, drops orders in the top of the huge bureaucratic machine under him, but little comes out at the bottom.

Indonesia is rich in oil, coal, metals, precious stones. Its waters teem with fish. Its jungles produce many valuable woods and every kind of animal life. Its fertile soil will grow rice, rubber, grain, and fruit. But most of this wealth is still undeveloped—even unexplored.

Many Indonesians, particularly on overpopulated Java, are small landholders or laborers who have been left destitute with the closing of the rubber plantations. These poverty-ridden peasants have looked to Sukarno's "guided democracy" for improvement; but since independence, Sukarno has had his hands full just holding his nation together, so diverse in race, language, and religion is it. The result: a claimed million card-carrying Communists, who could probably win an election if Sukarno permitted one. The Communist party has a simple program for the Indonesian workers and peasants: nationalization of the concession plantations, redistribution of land, higher and higher wages.

During the past year the Indonesians have pulled themselves together with unexpected and laudable vigor. The investment rate is now probably plus 3 or 4 per cent, a great improvement over the minus figure at which it stood two years ago. A number of rubber plantations are back in production, and oil production is healthy.

But it will be a decade, in my opinion, before free elections can be held, particularly in Java, without great danger of a Communist victory. We should be gratified that Sukarno seems to understand this, and is determined to use his "guided democracy" to prevent it.

Ghana: The First Steps

In Ghana, if anywhere in Africa, one might hope that democracy would take root and thrive. For here is relative prosperity ($160 a year per capita income), and here are comparatively high educational standards (about 15 per cent of the population in schools). Here is a country with more than half a billion dollars of reserves and no national debt; a country rich in agriculture (above all, cocoa) and minerals (iron, aluminum, gold, manganese). Furthermore, Ghana is small and compact enough (five million people in an area the size of Oregon) to be effectively administered. There is no special racial problem, since the .02-per-cent strong white minority owns no land, and accepts the status of temporary guests. There are no Communists within, or any foreign enemies without, to threaten independence and stability. Ghana's leaders are vigorous and well educated in the best schools of Britain and the United States.

I spent two days watching the Ghana Parliament, which is a miniature replica of that in London—complete with mace, white wigs, "Honorable" and "Right Honorable" gentlemen. I heard Opposition Leader Joe Appiah make a stirring speech in perfect Oxonian English. But, despite appearances, the fact is that democratic rights are currently being denied to many citizens of the new nation.

President Kwame Nkrumah today is trying to create the prerequisites and the machinery for a multiparty democracy. His first task has been to establish central authority over the country, and to maintain order. He is using the Convention People's party, of which he is leader for life, to intimidate and, where he deems it necessary, liquidate the opposition. His loyal politicos have chopped steadily away at the economic and political powers of the country's tribal chiefs, whose feudal prerogatives were incompatible with effective federal government.

Nkrumah is vigorous, but also ambitious and jealous of his power. He puts his head on coins, his statue in front of the Parliament building. He spends generously on all-African tours and conferences, in an attempt to consolidate for himself continental as well as national leadership. Many of Ghana's liberals and idealists are profoundly disturbed by the measures Nkrumah has taken against the opposition.

But my opinion coincides with those I heard frequently in Accra: Nkrumah's occasional petulance and arrogance are an acceptable price to pay for unity and the progress evident in Ghana's vigorous building program and its achievements in education.

India: The Great Question

Green parrots and monkeys play in the huge trees that line the road from Calcutta to Agra. It is an excellent road, built by the British, and improved by the Indian government since partition. Traffic is light—a few ancient buses, some trucks, a dozen cars an hour. At night jackals and deer run frightened from the headlights.

The highway passes many villages—miserable, reeking, run-down settlements of round or square mud huts, without doors or windows; of swarming, naked children with big stomachs; squealing pigs and scrawny cows; women in rags carrying water in earthen crocks on their heads from large round wells; mangy dogs looking for offal; cow-dung cakes plastered on walls, drying in the torrid sun for fuel.

There are signs of government activity in some villages—"Employment Exchange" and "Development Project"—but in many I saw little evidence of sustained effort to cultivate the soil. Near some villages, I saw people plowing with water buffaloes or bullocks. But the cornfields were untidy and filled with weeds; the rice was poor. Men squat beside the road, talking to one another, sometimes smoking—but, most frequently, just squatting. Seventy per cent of India's 380 million people live in these villages—these "dung heaps," as Nehru recently called them.

Indian employers, both industrial and agricultural, tend to be miserably backward, and so far have done little to improve matters. With some fifty million unemployed or underemployed ready to work for a few cents a day, why should they try? As Walter Reuther pointed out in several speeches he made in India in April 1956, Indian employers, by and large, know of only three ways to increase profits: cut wages, increase prices, reduce quality. In the absence of progressive management, Reuther told his labor audiences, it was up to them to take the initiative in increasing productivity so that they could get a larger slice of a larger pie. But the unions are new and have done little.

The Indian government is trying hard. It is dedicated to the principles of economic planning. The country's first Development Plan (1950-1955) stressed agriculture. By attaining self-sufficiency in basic foods, the government proposed to save foreign exchange and use it for industrialization. Achievements of the first Five Year Plan were substantial:

The food deficit was wiped out; the rationing system was abolished.

Electric lighting and the electrically driven water pump were introduced in ten thousand villages.

Average industrial production in organized industries was increased 50 per cent in five years.

The national income was raised by 18 per cent, to sixty dollars per capita annually.

Prices were held down, and the average Indian was able to buy a little more cloth and a little more food.

The second Five Year Plan provided for the industrialization of much of the Indian economy by 1960. Four steel mills, numerous large power plants, railroad car shops were to be built, and living standards were to improve. However, several things went wrong in the second Five Year Plan. First, there was a shortage of capital. The plan provided for the creation of "credit" to the extent of about $2.5 billion; and it anticipated receiving $1,680,000,000 in assistance from abroad, which did not materialize. In 1958 Indian Finance Minister Krishnamachari flew in desperation to the United States to try to get funds to make up some of his gaping four-billion-dollar shortfall.

Second, the industries built did not absorb labor as rapidly as it was entering the labor market. Unemployment grew. Food imports had to be resumed. When critics questioned the wisdom of trying under these conditions to industrialize so rapidly, government spokesmen replied that although the plan is ambitious, India cannot afford to go more slowly.

So, in the face of criticism both at home and abroad, the Indians are going ahead with their plans, counting on foreign aid as an important source of capital. Loans and grants from the United States, through the Colombo Plan, from private

American organizations, United Nations Technical Assistance, the International Bank for Reconstruction and Development, as well as from various foundations and charitable organizations, bring the total figure of Western public and private assistance to India for the last ten years close to a billion dollars. Soviet bloc credits for the same period amount to nearly a quarter billion dollars.

During the next several years, India will face a heavy food deficit which will threaten the country with bankruptcy, unless food production can be increased substantially. Some observers, including this writer, feel that under these conditions, the Third Five Year Plan should re-emphasize agriculture, even at the expense of dropping some of Nehru's grandiose heavy industrial projects. One specific prosposal, which I feel deserves more attention than it has received, is the following:

The United States agrees to allocate four billion dollars' worth of agricultural surpluses to India over four years. As soon as the Indian government gets this assurance, it borrows a billion dollars from its own banks; it hires five million unemployed Indians, and sets them to work clearing and plowing unused or fallow land, building major roads and fertilizer plants and similar projects—not building village schools or local roads, for this is the area of the Community Development Project. As the Indians are paid, they buy American surplus rice and wheat; and, with the money received, the Indian government then pays off its banks. At the end of several years, the Indian agricultural economy is substantially expanded, able to absorb labor, and produce more food.

However, the adoption of such projects is opposed by some Indians, who insist on concentrating every effort on heavy industry. In their impatience they overlook the fact that India's agriculture needs modernization rather than mechanization. Japan is the model rather than the United States, for, like Japan, India must absorb rather than save labor.

Although India with its fecundity has barely held its own in the area of economics, substantial achievements have been made in development.

And, certainly, India has earned a rousing cheer from the rest of the world for the way she has dealt with residual feudalism, and for her approach to the inequitable and uneconomic land-tenure system inherited from the British a decade ago. Without bloodshed or even serious coercion, some 600 sovereign princes were separated from their political power and most of their property, and pensioned off by a central government whose authority they thereby formally recognized. To accomplish this historic process, most European nations bled and sweated through revolutions and civil wars lasting generations.

Perhaps more important, India is quietly accomplishing an agrarian reform still overdue in Western countries like Italy and Spain. This land redistribution has been sparked by the peculiarly Indian Bhoodan Movement. Walking barefoot from village to village, Ghandian disciple Vinoba Bhave and his colleagues have been appealing to those with more land than they can use to give it to the landless; and nearly five million acres have already thus been contributed. The Bhoodan Movement has created a sense of responsibility in the minds of some landlords, fear in others, and has prepared the community psychologically to accept and implement land reform laws passed by most of India's states, limiting land holdings to from thirty to fifty acres (the current all-India average is under five); putting a ceiling of one-third of the crop on the rent to be charged for land; and providing for the buying of unused or surplus land by landless peasants for a fair price to be paid over a period of years.

Hand in hand with this agrarian reform, the Community Development Program has helped more than 300,000 of India's half million villages to build schools, roads, and other modern community requirements largely with their own hands.

India is also making violent attempts to make multiparty democracy work. The greatest praise is due to the country for successfully holding two general elections with a largely illiterate electorate. There are roughly fifty political parties in the Indian Republic, which is composed of twenty-nine constituent states. The Congress party is by far the strongest; although since the Socialist party split away from it in 1947, it has lost some ground. Dominated by veteran nationalists and haloed saints such as Nehru, the Congress party controls about 80 per cent of the power.

But the multiplicity of Indian parties actually offers very few alternatives to the miserably poor Indian seeking to better his condition. If he is dissatisfied with the Congress party rule, and blames it for his wretchedness, he can choose only between the well-organized Communist party and one of the small ineffectual parties like the Anti-Cow-Slaughter party. At the present time, the Communist party is gaining strength, and actually won a plurality in the State of Kerala.

The question today is whether India's multiparty democratic system can produce enough strong leadership to solve the country's overwhelming economic problems.

In the past, India has given birth to great leaders. As early as the sixth century B.C., there was Buddha; and from then on, for a dozen centuries, India was one of the great cultural centers of the world. In the third century B.C., Asoka, the great Buddhist emperor, unified virtually all of the subcontinent under one central administrative system. He then voluntarily renounced further military conquests and devoted himself to the welfare of his country. Trade flourished, and so did the arts and crafts, science and medicine.

More recently, India produced Ghandi and Nehru, both towering figures of our century. Nehru is India today. Like many other great leaders—Kemal Ataturk, Peter the Great, or Franklin Roosevelt—Nehru has shortcomings. He is sometimes irrational, vain, petulant, unreasonable. But, still and all, he is head and shoulders above his contemporaries in authority and stature —and, above all, he believes in India.

When I asked Nehru whether he was apprehensive about the

centrifugal forces created by the linguistic states and their region-alism, he had this to say:

Yes, we have centrifugal forces; but, in politics as in physics, for each centrifugal force there is a centripetal force. When we were struggling for our freedom, the struggle kept us together, united. Now that we have achieved freedom, of course we have disagree-ments; and we bicker about things. But we are essentially united now. True, we have our problems, but I am not apprehensive about this one. . . . Others are more difficult, more complex. The modern-ization of our villages and of agriculture, the building of industries, education. . . . We are doing things. But there is so much still to do, so frightfully much. . . .

Placing his hopes in the wisdom of his ancient though largely unlettered race, and in the help of the world's "have" nations, Nehru is making a brilliant attempt to solve his country's prob-lems without forced labor, concentration camps, and the other paraphernalia of totalitarianism, the methods with which the Chinese Communists are attacking similar problems. Behind Nehru stand younger men. Two who impressed me very much are S. K. Dey and Minoo Masani, men who may carry forward Nehru's efforts when he passes on. Though their chances of success in solving their economic problems democratically, and maintaining free institutions without the Communists' using these institutions to seize power, are at best, I venture, fifty-fifty, the United States and the West must make every effort to help them try.

These few examples indicate how close the margin is in the Hungry World between failure and success, between bank-ruptcy and solvency, life and death.

Four ⊘ *Why Democracy Is Not Enough*

Beneath the varied patchwork pattern of local and regional problems harassing the Hungry World lie several fundamental issues which must be faced and dealt with. The first and most fundamental is fertility.

Population Pressure

Population increase is a world problem, but one most pressing in the underdeveloped areas for a double reason: birth rates are higher, while resources are fewer.

I was present recently at a budget discussion. Public-health officials of one of the newer nations in the Hungry World were trying to decide how to allocate the limited funds at their disposal among the many areas of their activity: pediatrics, public hygiene, maternity, infectious diseases, mental health, research, and so on. It was all too clear that it would be years before the country had the funds and the forces to deal adequately with all phases of the nation's health problems; in the meantime, it was the responsibility of these officials to decide what to include and what to leave out or what to underemphasize in their program. One official suggested that care of the newly born and the very old be underemphasized because "the very old will die

93

soon anyhow, while the most economical time to have children die is at birth."

Although several people in the group recoiled at the phrase, the majority agreed that the proposal should be adopted. A few others present pointed out that it would be far more economical to restrict birth to that number which could be fed and cared for with available resources. But this issue was dropped because of the vigor with which several men present objected to birth control as a matter of religious principle.

Of course the problem of population pressure is more severe in some places than others. Japan, China, India, and Java are four areas where grave pressures already exist. Only in Japan have any effective measures been taken to reduce the birth rate, and there it has been done largely by making abortions legal and nearly free, a crude and painful way which has achieved a fall in the population increase coefficient from about 1.9 to about 0.9 in a decade.

A generation of effort in India under the direction of Lady Rama Ran achieved no appreciable results. In China and Java no serious attempts have been made. Perhaps the new hormone pills currently being tested in Puerto Rico herald a major technological break-through and will make possible the reduction of the birth rate in each country to some figure commensurable with available resources. But this will be possible only if the principle of birth control wins general acceptance. In this respect the Roman Catholics stand alone as the only sizable group, and one with great power in Western capitals, which rejects the only procedure which could prevent the birth of babies precondemned to die of starvation, exposure, and neglect. For regionally this is already occurring.

True, new agricultural techniques and the use of plankton and synthetics may increase the world's food production substantially. But one-twentieth of the human beings who have ever lived are alive today, and our number is increasing by roughly fifty million a year. It took over 200,000 years for our planet's population to reach 2.5 billion. Now in only thirty years our number will increase by two billion more. By 1962 the world will have three billion people; by 1977, four billion. The year 2000 will see us six billion strong unless some catastrophe occurs to alter existing trends. We are dealing with a geometric progression. It will not be long before we will have no room to stand.

I can only hope that the Roman Catholic Church finds it possible to review its position on this important issue as it has in the past reviewed other positions in the light of new developments, so that the Western world at least can try to deal realistically with this problem.

Education

A second general problem faced by all the Hungry World is education. Just to begin the monumental task of teaching the illiterate millions to read and write requires, in the first place, an army of teachers, most of whom can be part-time volunteers.

At the same time, provisions must be made to make elementary education available to the younger quarter of the population. This will require school buildings and minimal classroom materials and books and a corps of professional teachers.

Then a small but growing group of the more gifted and ambitious must be given opportunities at secondary and higher education.

At the same time, another group, probably at first much more numerous, must be given vocational training.

All four aspects of this job must be carried out at the same time and will require major expenditures of money and energy. Already many of the Hungry World's new nations have made startling progress. Indonesia, backward and harassed in other ways, has during the past decade increased its adult literacy from about 15 per cent to perhaps 40 per cent.

I visited schools in India and Indonesia, in North Africa and

Korea, in Pakistan and Nigeria. The buildings were often far from adequate. In Tunisia shrines had been requisitioned for emergency use. Near Madras we saw classes being held under the trees, pending the construction of a school building. In many areas regional resistance is acute: in northern Nigeria and in much of the Moslem Middle East parents are loath to let their daughters go even to elementary schools. South Africa's Bantu Education Act resulted in closing excellent mission schools which, the Afrikaaners felt, were sowing dangerous seeds in native minds.

But everywhere the children seemed avid for educational opportunities denied their parents and now becoming available. This elementary education, now widely enjoyed, spells social revolution in many parts of the Hungry World, where the prejudices and privileges of the past will not survive universal education any more than they will universal suffrage.

Education is thus the most important single prerequisite for the eventual operation of an effective political democracy. No dictatorship, colonial or indigenous, can, I believe, justify its existence if it does not make substantial efforts toward popular education. As a target I think it is fair to say that under-developed nations should put at least 5 per cent of their gross product into education.

It is in the area of education that the underdeveloped nations most need outside assistance—teachers, administrators, books, equipment, and scholarships.

Although regional variations are to be expected, I believe that until the adult literacy rate in any nation reaches 50 per cent, there can be no serious talk of operative democracy.

Capital

A third general problem before the Hungry World is lack of capital—the machinery, equipment, and trained personnel needed to increase the production of everything from vegetables to machines.

The reason for the importance of capital at the present time is clear. During the past two generations modern medicine and sanitary engineering have cleared the way for the demographic explosion described above. Traditional agricultural and fishing techniques cannot adequately feed the people who already live in most of Asia and Africa and much of Latin America, let alone the 2- to 3-per-cent annual increase. Existing production cannot even give them that subsistence livelihood their parents endured, let alone provide them with the new things that the post World War II revolution in expectations has led them to demand —schools, shoes, shirts, metal implements, and outboard motors.

Most of the Hungry World's citizens, like nineteenth-century socialists, are more engrossed with distributing wealth than with creating it. But the ablest of them realize that it is not so much the size of the slices as the size of the pie that is the determining factor in the realization of their hopes.

For wealth must be produced before it can be distributed. And the governments of the new nations of the Hungry World are today harassed with the necessity to borrow, beg, confiscate, procure, or produce the capital to modernize their economies in order to produce enough to give their people what they need and demand. These governments often rise and fall depending on their success at finding the capital to do the things that need doing.

What needs doing? I would like to break down the areas of public and private investment into four basic categories.

WHAT NEEDS DOING

First and most fundamental is the modernization of the production of food. This means dams and canals for irrigation; the manufacture or importation of metal ploughs and other implements; the production and distribution of fertilizers and improved seeds; better breeds of domestic birds and animals; the introduction of crop rotation, which in turn means some agricultural extension work. In the fishing industry improvements depend on better boats and nets, improved methods, and the use of motors. In order to transport food from the places where it is produced to the people who need it, the Hungry World needs bridges, roads, vehicles, canals, boats, and barges, as well as the communications needed for their effective operation.

In most of the world's underdeveloped countries the improved production and distribution of food is the first charge on investment and can absorb large quantities of capital over a number of years in both the public and private sectors.

The second area in which capital is needed is in the construction of schools and the training of teachers, mentioned above. These investments fall almost entirely in the public sector.

The third area of capital investment is in the discovery, development, and production of raw materials—minerals, fuels, and timber. In most cases these materials cannot at first be processed in the underdeveloped country itself, but are exported. In some fortunate underdeveloped countries mineral wealth is such that its exploitation can go far toward financing the development of the entire economy as it is now doing in the Union of South Africa (gold, iron, coal, diamonds), Northern Rhodesia (copper) and Malaya (tin). Outside capital for the development of these resources is usually available in the private sector without great effort on the part of the underdeveloped country, although during recent years world surpluses of such items as copper and petroleum have made the big companies unwilling to invest large sums of developmental capital except under concession conditions which the hypersensitive and suspicious new governments are often unwilling to accept. For example, as noted, currently Brazil continues to spend most of its coffee money on petroleum products, while its own oil stays in the ground for lack of capital.

The fourth area of investment in underdeveloped areas is in manufacture. Here the need is immense and diverse in every

country, and investment and development can go on for decades
or generations as the savages or subsistence farmers of yesterday
become producers and consumers and, finally, owners and investors.

SOURCES OF CAPITAL

Capital can be obtained in several ways. It can be stolen or
borrowed from someone else who has it, or it can be accumulated slowly by producing more than one consumes and saving
the difference.

The British, who first ran into the problem on a large scale,
did all three. They stole from Spanish and Portuguese merchants
and freebooters (who had stolen from the Incas and others).
They borrowed from their own aristocrats. And, most important,
they engaged for a century in what Karl Marx called primitive
capital accumulation or, as most contemporary economists know
it, forced saving. Hundreds of thousands of English farmers
were driven by the repeal of the Corn Laws and other measures
from the land into the new industrial cities, where they were
forced for survival to work twelve and fourteen hours a day in
factories and coal mines—boys and girls of eight and ten along
with their parents—while living on a bare subsistence level in
squalor and destitution. It was their conditions, graphically described by Charles Dickens and Thomas Hardy, that moved
Karl Marx to utter his famed and at one time accurate slogan:
"Workers . . . you have nothing to lose but your chains."

For three or four generations the British produced a great
deal, consumed just a little, and the difference went to pay for
the railroads, mines, factories, and ships that formed the skeleton
of British industrial power. Gradually capital surpluses accumulated in the banks of London so that, as other nations—Holland,
France, Germany—began their periods of capital formation,
the British became investors.

Thus it was that when the United States began intensive industrialization after the Civil War, we were saved many of the

horrors the British had gone through a century earlier by the billions of investment dollars which flowed into the United States from London and from Paris and from Amsterdam to finance the construction of our railroads and steel mills. In any single year during the 1880's or 1890's, more than half the net capital invested in the United States economy came from abroad. Some of the investors, of course, lost all in bursting bubbles and fancy swindles, or simply as the result of bad judgment. But most of them received handsome dividends, which annually flowed back to Europe in the form of cotton and furs, gold and timber. Some sensitive Americans resented this "exploitation" by foreign capitalists, but most Americans realized that if the dividends went back to the old country, the steel mills and railroads stayed and formed the basis of America's future industrial power. America remained a net recipient of foreign investments until 1914.

Russia faced a similar situation at the turn of the present century. Large quantities of British, French, Belgian, and some American capital were invested in Russia before World War I. Some three billion dollars went into railroad construction alone. Then came the Bolshevik Revolution. Foreign as well as domestic investments were expropriated, and a generation of Russians was forced under the most oppressive coercion to work long and hard while consuming a bare minimum to pay for the Five Year plans. In this as in other respects the Communist government in Moscow exploited its population as Marx described the capitalists' treatment of their workers: subsistence on that bare minimum of food, clothing, and shelter necessary for them to be able to continue to work and raise a new generation.

By mid-century the Russians had begun to accumulate capital surpluses which they in their turn are now investing on their own peculiar terms in countries like China, Afghanistan, and India. Today the countries of the whole Hungry World face the same problem that confronted the Russians a generation ago, the

United States three generations ago, and the British before that. They need capital.

DIRECT ACQUISITION

Many of the world's new governments are not above stealing and did indeed engage in nationalization and confiscation on occasion. The Indian government simply seized the fabulous wealth of some of the maharajas as well as nationalizing such institutions as the insurance companies.

Governments which emerged after wars, civil wars, or revolutions often simply took the property of their defeated enemies. In this way Japanese assets all over Asia were confiscated; the Indonesian Government took over many Dutch assets; and the Algerians are now announcing their intention to repudiate concessions granted by the French today for the development of Sahara oil.

As colonies won their independence, they often claimed title to the property of the former colonial power and its nationals.

Land reforms were implemented in most new nations, but in nearly all non-Communist areas the reformed landlords were compensated to some measure, and the reform itself was a redistribution of wealth rather than capital formation.

Most non-Communist governments hesitated to confiscate or nationalize the assets of major foreign investors, public and private, for fear that it would damage their credit rating and make it difficult for them to do business in the future.

So that, for most nations of the Hungry World, stealing did not constitute a bountiful source of investment capital.

The picture is very different in the Communist countries— Red China, North Korea, and North Viet-Nam. Here the governments confiscated without compensation the property of all foreign and most domestic investors, all the assets of their own wealthy, most of whom fled or were killed. The property of the urban middle class was acquired by the nationalization of their businesses and that of the middle peasantry by the land reform.

Most recently and spectacularly, the government in Peking is taking the houses, tools, and even the pots and pans of the entire peasantry as they enter the communes in one of history's most massive shakedowns.

PRIMITIVE CAPITAL ACCUMULATION

Most governments in the Hungry World lack the desire or the political fanaticism to squeeze their own populations as the British working classes were squeezed in the eighteenth century. And even if they wanted to do it, they would have trouble. For this is, after all, the century of the common man and the eight-seven-six-hour day. Two generations of Western liberals have been writing books about the iniquities of economic serfdom, and the ideas in them have become widely accepted and written into legislation all over the world.

True, in the Union of South Africa and to a lesser degree in Rhodesia, native mine workers are today being pushed to high productivity for a low wage, but this may end in bloody revolt, as I have indicated elsewhere in these pages. In most of the Hungry World labor legislation which the economies can ill afford restricts the rate of saving to a low level indeed, while in some countries like Bolivia it has kept the economy in a state of net disinvestment for years.

The masses, intoxicated with the prospect or the reality of freedom, have been misled by their own intellectuals into the belief that this freedom itself can through some painless process make them rich. This, added to the fact that in much of the Hungry World the masses are both undernourished and unaccustomed to work, adds up to low productivity.

Even when the Asian or African through luck or unusual effort acquires money, he tends to spend it on some consumer item—food and drink, clothing, jewelry, or some new toy like a radio set—rather than invest it himself or give it to a bank or insurance company to invest for him.

In this connection the importance of banks as instruments of capital formation in the Hungry World can hardly be overestimated. It is most unfortunate that they are so few, that good Moslems do not believe in interest at all, and that the Communists have succeeded in many areas in defaming banks as instruments of foreign imperialism and exploitation.

If most of the Hungry World has been unable to save much investment capital, the Communists have been astonishingly effective in this respect. For the Communists are the Calvinists of Asia and Africa. They work hard themselves and drive their people ruthlessly.

To be sure, there is a legal eight-hour working day in China. But in every shop and office some hero volunteers to work twelve hours and shames his comrades into similar efforts under pain of social and perhaps even administrative pressure. Evenings and on days of rest millions "volunteer" to work on dams and canals or stoking backyard blast furnaces to make needed iron, later condemned as unfit for industrial use.

Nor do the masses in Communist countries have any opportunity to squander the product of their labor on whims or frivolities. The collectives and communes see that consumption is limited to bare necessities, while production is kept at a peak. The urban masses are kept in hand by a planned economy which exports vast quantities of food and consumer goods, leaving the population to queue up for what is left. Other methods of restricting consumption: voluntary state bond subscriptions, high prices, low wages.

While some fifty millions of unemployed Indians squat stoically on their haunches in freedom and penury, every man, woman, and child in China is kept busy to the point of exhaustion. The economic result of this comparative situation is predictable.

INVESTMENTS FROM OUTSIDE

Desperately short of capital which they are unable to steal or to squeeze from their own economy, the new nations of the

Hungry World are trying to borrow. They are trying to persuade foreign investors to lend them the money to build factories and dams. In some cases they agree to allow foreign concessionaires to build and operate enterprises in their countries, though pressures are now heavy against such "sale of a nation's wealth" to concessionaires.

In this effort Communist countries have not done nearly so well as their competitors. Russia removed two billion dollars' worth of industrial equipment from Manchuria in 1945 as "war booty," later sent some of it back as "economic aid" to China. Extensive Soviet loans and grants to China, North Korea, and North Viet-Nam will be described in the next chapter, but they fall far short of the needs of the recipients.

The sixty-odd non-Communist countries of Asia, Africa, and Latin America have received substantial sums of capital since World War II. It has been in the form of direct aid, military and nonmilitary, private investment, loans and grants, programs organized by foundations, reinvested profits on old investments, gifts from religious organizations, technical aid, and the training of personnel in foreign schools.

Of course not all this aid constitutes capital formation. Much of it is consumed; much of it goes to nonproductive military establishments.

AFRICA

Since World War II both private and public enterprises in Africa have received substantial funds from abroad. Nearly half a billion dollars came from the World Bank; and more than two billion dollars from French government development funds, British Colonial Development Corporation funds, and the United States. In addition to all this, the Soviet Union has committed $565 million in Egypt; and the Common Market countries have agreed to pump about one billion dollars (mostly from West Germany) into French Africa. Reinvestments are heavy, particularly in the Congo and in Rhodesia, and the investment rate of domestic savings in the Union and the Federation and Kenya is high.

The total book value of United States private investments in Africa is less than half a billion dollars, not an impressive figure. But other countries are doing better, and best figures indicate that the total capital investments in Africa are now running between four and five billion dollars a year, or between 15 and 20 per cent of the continent's gross product—an average well above that for the Western world.

LATIN AMERICA

Foreign investments in Latin America are running about one billion dollars annually, roughly half of it from the United States. Total United States investments in Latin America are about eight billion dollars, and much of this represents profits reinvested over a long period of time.

Direct aid to Latin America has been small and limited largely to Bolivia. On the other hand, the United States Government gets about $100 million a year as taxes on incomes from United States investments in Latin America, and the annual profit on United States investments in Latin America is substantially greater than new investments. This is the economics behind the stones thrown at Mr. Nixon in 1958.

It is clear that this situation is unhealthy and that resentful Latin Americans will be tempted to rectify the imbalance by heavier taxes and perhaps nationalization.

MIDDLE EAST

Foreign investments in the Middle East are extensive, but hard to evaluate because of the complexity of international oil operations. I have heard them estimated at ten billion dollars. Certain it is that the profits on Mid-East oil currently run at about two billion dollars a year, of which the Mid-East governments get about half. The plow-back by the oil companies, which must be considered as new investment, as its expatriation is provided for by agreement and by law, amounts to more than half a billion dollars a year.

But little developmental capital investment has found its way to the Middle East, most of whose economy remains backward, while the huge profits from the oil industry are often squandered by a handful of feudal sheiks who care little for their hungry subjects.

Public sector aid, military and nonmilitary, has been heavy to Turkey, Iran, Jordan, and Saudi Arabia, totals perhaps one billion dollars a year, while the United Nations spends more than half its total budget feeding a million Arab refugees in Palestine.

ASIA

Capital investment in Asia has been small considering the area's population.

The United States has been spending about one billion dollars a year in direct economic aid and about as much again in military aid—$700 million a year in Korea alone. United States aid has been an important factor in the economies of Cambodia, Formosa, Laos, and Viet-Nam.

Straight private investment has been small, and that has gone mostly to Indonesia, the Philippines, and India.

The World Bank has made some money available to Asia and so have Britain and Canada through the Colombo Plan.

ALLOCATION OF INVESTMENTS

Bitter arguments take place among the new nations' leaders as to how to allocate investment efforts. Many feel that the first necessity in much of Asia and Africa is improved diet. These leaders would like to spend available funds for food, such as wheat, meat, rice, oils, in order to raise living standards.

Others believe that economic development is problem number one. But opinions differ on whether to invest first in light or heavy industry. Some statesmen advocate maximizing capital investment in heavy industries and allowing living standards to keep their present low level for a long time. Into this category falls President Nasser, with his steel mill just south of Cairo. Others would like to see capital investment channeled first into agriculture, mining, and light industry. This point of view is based on the sound thesis that in these sectors of the economy a given sum of capital invested produces a maximum return in the shortest time and also creates more new jobs. All other things being equal, my sympathies lie with the latter group. But local conditions vary so much that generalization is difficult.

NEW NATIONS' DILEMMA

In this connection the youngest nations of Africa and Asia face a special problem. One reason why their domestic saving rates, hence their domestic capital investment rates, are relatively high is that living standards are so low. What will happen when independence, trade-union activity, and social development force up abysmally low wages? Investment rates will tend to fall, retarding economic development. If these new governments are wise, they will try to increase productivity more rapidly than wages. Politically, this will be difficult. Furthermore, if these governments want continued outside investments, they will have to maintain high rates of profit on investments already made and resist the temptation to expropriate or nationalize industries already in existence. This also may prove politically difficult, particularly in areas where leftists are pressing for nationalization.

As new nations achieve independence and the economic umbilical cords are cut, they tend to lose those resources formerly received from such organizations as FIDES and the Commonwealth Development Fund. At the same time domestic pressures will tend to diminish local capital investments. This modern version of Russia's classical economic "scissors" threatens in the next decade to cut the currently healthy high investment rate in most of Africa precisely when its maintenance is of major importance.

This danger is intensified by the fact that newly independent nations are facing three new demands on their resources: first, the creation of adequate educational systems, which they desperately need; second, the creation of armies, which they do not need at all but demand to bolster their prestige and to bulwark the power of their leaders; third, the diversification of vulnerable one-crop economies.

All these forces, incidentally, are currently present with classic simplicity in Ghana. That country's healthy capital formation rate comes principally from the profits on cocoa sales. When the British ran the country, they kept cocoa prices down in Ghana, while collecting as much as possible from foreign purchasers, and used the profits for roads and other improvements in the country and for dividends to foreign shareholders.

Currently, Nkrumah faces popular demand for higher prices to the cocoa growers. If he gives way, fewer funds will be available for education and economic development. An unfettered parliamentary opposition in Ghana, besides expressing the interests of the feudal chiefs, would inevitably demand more money for cocoa; and, granted the unsophisticated level of Ghana's population, this money would be spent largely on consumer goods rather than on roads and power plants, to the detriment of Ghana's economic development. Aware of this, Nkrumah is now moving against the opposition with measures often characterized as unconstitutional. I personally feel that this policy is justifiable in terms of Ghana's economic welfare. Somebody must keep Ghanian consumption increases below production increases—and Dr. Nkrumah is doing it. If he spends some of the revenue putting conspicuous bronze statues of himself around Accra, it is in bad taste, but I think Dr. Nkrumah is worth it.

UNITED STATES INVESTMENTS

The United States private sector contribution to Hungry World capital formation is not so great as it could or should be.

In 1957 American investors got $3.75 billion in profits on their $25.3 billions of investments abroad. New United States investments abroad amounted to about five billion dollars—just over 1 per cent of our GNP. Fifty per cent of it went to Europe and Canada. Less than 9 per cent of our direct private investments are in the critical areas of Asia and Africa.

United States Government programs—military and nonmilitary—amounted to some five billion dollars, to which private charities and foundation programs add another billion. The public sector of our expenditures in the Hungry World is already far greater than the private sector. In this area we have already become more than half "socialist," at least in part because private capital dragged its feet.

But even if United States investments in the Hungry World were doubled—and I should like to see this happen—the demand would not be satisfied.

The nations of the Hungry World must have capital enough to raise per capita income annually by at least 2 per cent. If they do not get it from the West, the temptation to turn to Moscow for aid and even to adopt communism will constitue a constantly increasing threat to us.

The Hungry World needs, and the United States can and should undertake, a vast new program of capital investment.

Government

The fourth general problem the Hungry World faces is administrative. Even before achieving independence, the new nations face the task of governing themselves. Laws must be enacted and enforced, taxes must be levied and collected, municipal services maintained, order secured.

This task is the more complex because most of the Hungry World has no experience in self-government in the modern sense of the phrase.

The restraints and behavior patterns of family and faith and tribe held together the loose-knit societies of most of Asia and much of Africa and Latin America before the arrival of the colonial powers. Now, after several generations of alien rule and after fundamental and irreversible economic and social alterations, these nations find themselves self-governing, even independent. In exuberant bursts of enthusiastic nationalism they sometimes cast off the administrative institutions of colonial administration, leaving nothing but the rusty residue of old and atavistic tribal bodies to cope with the problems of government.

The position of the Western powers has been that democracy should furnish the answer to these problems. We have tended to measure the success of these new nations by the degree to which they contrived to create institutions like our own. Often we have sent teams of political scientists to help them draft constitutions and organize governmental institutions.

These well-meaning efforts are often based on the assumption that democracy will work in the Hungry World. It is my opinion that this assumption will not stand up under critical examination. I believe that there is some basis for Fidel Castro's statement in April 1959 that elections in Cuba would be disastrous if held before "we do away with unemployment, illiteracy and misery . . ." His implicit reasons are clear: the people would vote against the government because they are not yet able to exercise intelligent discrimination in voting.

I believe that countries with per capita incomes under $200 a year and adult literacy rates under 50 per cent cannot be expected to govern themselves democratically.

This sounds arbitrary, and indeed it is. Conditions and traditions vary from country to country. Germany, with a high literacy rate and a per capita income close to a thousand dollars a year made a mess of democracy in the 1930's. India—far below my minima—is making a valiant and impressive attempt at democratic government. But I believe these exceptions are due to extraordinary conditions.

Let me try to prove my thesis on several planes. The first is local administration.

TRADITION

The tribal societies of Africa, Asia, and Latin America—and of North America, too—were governed by some variant of the following system.

A tribe had a chief (sheikh, caid, emir, sultan), usually hereditary, surrounded and aided by a council of elders—also usually hereditary. When an issue of importance arose, it was discussed by the council of elders, usually presided over by the chief, with great candor. Varied viewpoints were expressed. Astrologers, medicine men, and other experts were summoned to give counsel. Then, at a certain point, usually without any voting and invariably without recorded votes, the chief reached a decision. From then on it was treason for any member of the tribe to question his decision or reopen the issue. When a chief repeatedly made unsound decisions, the council of elders poisoned or exiled him and found another chief.

This is the way most human beings were governed in tribal societies. The concept of a popular election was dangerous radicalism. The institution of the loyal opposition, that magnificent invention of the British, was unknown. No votes were taken. Decisions were "unanimous." An individual (or a small self-perpetuating oligarchy) sat at the apex of an administrative pyramid with complete control over the area involved until he stubbed his toe on some issue. Then he was pushed aside in favor of a new chief.

This is essentially the way in which the Soviet Union is governed under "democratic centralism." It is close to the way Communist China is run under Mao's People's Democratic Dictatorship. In much of the Hungry World the concept of voted decisions, with recorded minority votes and opposition criticism of state decisions, all of which may appeal to local intellectuals trained in the University of Chicago, the Sorbonne, and the London School of Economics, seems strange and inapplicable to the still illiterate masses, for whom "democracy" is a concept too abstract to grasp. They are accustomed to follow and obey men rather than principles. Often they confuse personal liberty with political freedom.

For these masses some form of dictatorship—or, to use *Pravda's* terminology, "people's democracy"—may be both more understandable and more appropriate than multiparty parliamentary democracy.

ECONOMIC DEVELOPMENT

As we saw earlier in this argument, underdeveloped countries need high capital formation rates if they are to survive.

There is a question as to whether a heavy investment rate can be achieved in a retarded country under a multiparty democracy. One African prime minister of what will soon be an independent country expressed to me his doubts on this matter as follows:

I will go before my constituents on the eve of elections and say, "Vote for me, and we will build this new hydroelectric power station. We will invest in it so-and-so many millions of our nation's wealth, and in ten years we will be producing so-and-so many kilowatts of power. Then we will build light industries, and in due course you, my friends, will have bicycles."

Then the opposition leader will appear. "Vote for me," he will say, "and we will forget all about this silly power plant. Instead of wasting the people's time and money on that, we will buy new British-made bicycles for all of you right after elections."

I know my people well enough to fear that under these circumstances they would vote for the opposition, thus condemning our nation to permanent penury because we will not be forming capital rapidly enough to provide for necessary healthy development.

Impressed with this African's argument, I asked men everywhere I went whether they thought democracy was workable in their country. The affirmative answers I got tended to be from young idealists who thought democracy would work because it *should* work. Men of experience tended to answer in the negative.

In the words of one knighted British official to whom I put the question: "My government believes in democracy. My own belief is that it might perhaps work better here if we did away with this business of voting and suspended, at least temporarily, the institution of the opposition."

To generalize: In countries with literacy rates under 50 per cent and per capita incomes under $200 a year, a multiparty democracy cannot provide a rate of savings, a regime of austerity, diligence, and investment necessary for healthy economic growth.

Obviously, inspired leadership and a population, wise and disciplined though illiterate and poor, might make possible exceptions. But unfortunately, most leaders in the new nations are not inspired. On the contrary, many of them think of their own assumption of power as the essence of freedom. Their citizens are harder to please. They demand order and prosperity. When they do not get these things, they become disappointed and angry.

THE CATEGORICAL ALTERNATIVE

With a stiff bow to Emanuel Kant, I should like at this point to articulate a thesis of major importance in all areas of the Hungry World where Communist parties exist and operate.

As I have indicated above, the masses in the Hungry World remain grindingly poor, though their appetites and aspirations have been whetted to a high point of desire. Impatient, they are often ready to rebel against their governments because they are corrupt and inefficient or simply because they are their governments. When given the freedom to speak, organize, and vote, they "vote the rascals out."

This thesis applies to the Communist as well as the non-Communist countries. For no government in the Hungry World today can form capital rapidly enough to create the industries and products their populations want. If the masses of South Viet-Nam were given democratic freedom, I believe they would vote out President Ngo Dinh Diem. If the North Viet-Namese were free to do so, they would vote out their Communist government, and for identical reasons.

I hasten to make several exceptions to this hypothesis: Japan, the Philippines, Hong Kong, Singapore, Israel, Lebanon, Turkey, perhaps Tunisia, and several countries in Latin America. These countries have literacy rates above 50 per cent, per capita incomes of more than $200 a year. These people can perhaps analyze their problems and make reasonable decisions. Here democracy may work.

In all the rest of the Hungry World the words of French philosopher Pierre Proudhon—intended to apply to another age —seem pertinent: "Universal suffrage means revolution."

The Communist governments of Asia recognize and deal with this reality by denying their masses freedoms of speech, press, and organization, thus preventing opposition activities. When opposition does appear, the Communist governments eliminate it by social surgery so drastic as to discourage others who might be inclined in the same direction.

In the non-Communist areas some governments, in ignorance or naïvete and encouraged by the West, have tried to implement democracy in their lands. Dissident individuals are relatively free to speak, to form groups and parties, to publish newspapers, to criticize their governments, and to accept aid and guidance from abroad.

In many of these countries Communists are winning elections and influence, not because their masses have become Communists, but simply because they are in impatient rebellion against their governments and the Communists constitute the "other party."

Were a real and complete democratic process to be applied in these young nations, things might still work out. An inefficient or corrupt government would be voted out of power in favor of an opposition party, which would then have its chance to do better. If and when it failed, the voters could change again as they have done throughout so many years of history in Western Europe and North America.

But the advent of Communist theory dedicated to the concept of class dictatorship, and the existence of the Soviet Union and China to dominate, guide, and utilize the activities of Communist parties in other countries, render this process impossible. Once in power the Communists simply do not allow themselves to be voted out.

To use a mundane analogy, a poker game is really not a poker game when one player has no money and his opponent has unlimited funds. The latter need win only one hand, and the game is over.

This thesis is currently demonstrating its validity in a number of places in Asia. Had not the government of Indonesia wisely postponed the elections in Java in 1959, the Communists would have won them, not because the Javanese peasants have become Marxist-Leninists but because they are poor and unhappy. The Communists won an election in Kerala and may well win in 1960 in Madras and Bengal because the unhappy masses are fed up with the Congress party and the Communists present the most plausible alternative.

Let me illustrate this thesis with a quotation from South Viet-Nam's President Diem: "The vital issue is to establish an effective state apparatus. . . . A weak and powerless executive will bring about discontent and indignation. . . . This might pave the way for Revolution. . . . A strong and efficient executive organization capable of rapidly solving the complex and urgent problems . . . is a guarantee for the democratic regime. . . ."

Africa is far away from communism's base of operations and so far has few serious Communist parties. But they will make their appearance, I am afraid, before the 50 per cent-$200 point is reached. Latin America, even farther from Moscow and Peking and more developed, may miss the consequences of my thesis, which in its barest form might be formulated thus:

In underdeveloped areas democracy produces communism.

WHO SHOULD VOTE?

When the United States was emerging into self-government and toward independence, our electoral laws gave one adult in seven the vote. After the reforms of 1832 in England, one adult in five was given the vote. It was 1919 before Britain and the United States achieved universal adult suffrage, and as a Federal investigation committee in Alabama discovered in 1958, there may still be areas in the United States where the franchise is withheld from certain of our citizens.

Today the franchise is being rapidly extended throughout the Hungry World. In countries like Kenya the slogan "one man, one vote" has become popular. I would guess that within five years Kenya will have a legislative council elected by universal adult franchise. Kenya's level of education and economic development today can be perhaps compared with the Britain of King John, when universal franchise was still centuries away.

The validity of this thesis in Southeast Asia is widely recognized by knowledgeable observers. For example, Alexis Johnson, United States Ambassador to Thailand, recently wrote: "It is hardly surprising that European-style parliamentary democracy has been something less than a success in this part of the world."

For indeed, what kind of legislation can we expect to emerge from a general election in Kenya? At best it would be amorphous and unwieldy. At worst, it would be anarchic.

I expressed these thoughts to one of Africa's most talented young leaders in Nairobi. "Of course we are for universal suffrage *now*," he said. "But it is very clear that for some time we are going to have to be very careful whom we allow the people of Kenya to vote for. It is also clear that for some time a small disciplined elite party is going to have to guide our institutions, to lead our country through the period of education and rapid capital formation necessary to prepare our people for effective democracy."

Nor is this idea new. British Labor party leader Aneurin Bevan, after a serious study of the development of his country, wrote:

Democracy as we know it today is the product of the 20th century. . . . It is highly doubtful that the achievements of the Industrial Revolution would have been permitted if the franchise had been universal. It is very doubtful because a great deal of the capital aggregations that we are at present enjoying are the results of the wages that our fathers went without. . . .

This reasoning seems to me eminently sensible and applies today in most of the countries of the Hungry World. It constitutes another demonstration of the validity of my thesis: Democracy cannot be expected to work in countries with less than 50 per cent adult literacy and less than $200 a year per capita income.

Let us now list the countries of the Hungry World, with their indices of literacy and affluence and see where democracy may be expected to work.

Country	*Per Capita Income*[1] (*$ Per Year*)	*Illiteracy*[2] *Rate*
Afghanistan	-100 (100 or less)	95-99
Algeria	250	80-85
Angola	-100	95-99
Argentina	450	10-15
Basutoland	-100	45-50
Bechuanaland	-100	75-80
Bolivia	-100	65-70
Brazil	220	50-55
Burma	50	40-45
Cambodia	70	80-85

Country	Per Capita Income[1] ($ Per Year)	Illiteracy[2] Rate
Cameroons (U.K.)	-100	90-95
Ceylon	175	35-40
Chile	320	20-25
China (Mainland)	60	50-55
Colombia	250	45-50
Congo	50	60-65
Costa Rica	210	20-25
Ecuador	150	40-45
Egypt	130	75-80
El Salvador	180	60-65
Ethiopia	60	95-99
French Equatorial Africa	85	95-99
French West Africa	95	95-99
Gambia	-100	90-95
Ghana	160	75-80
Guatemala	150	70-75
Honduras	140	60-65
Hong Kong	250	40-45
India	60	80-85
Indonesia	70	80-85
Iran	150	85-90
Iraq	150	85-90
Israel	560	5-10
Japan	260	2- 3
Jordan	-100	80-85
Kenya	75	75-80
Korea	81	60-65
Laos	50	80-85
Lebanon	350	50-55
Liberia	-100	90-95
Libya	110	90-95
Madagascar	110	65-70
Malaya	350	60-65
Mexico	215	35-40
Morocco	110	85-90
Mozambique	70	95-99
Nicaragua	160	60-65
Nigeria	60	85-90

Country	Per Capita Income[1] ($ Per Year)	Illiteracy[2] Rate
Pakistan	-100	80-85
Panama	300	30-35
Peru	140	50-55
Philippines	200	35-40
Rhodesias	120	75-80
Saudi Arabia	-100	95-99
Sierra Leone	-100	90-95
Singapore	400	50-55
Somaliland (Ital.)	-100	95-99
Sudan	-100	90-95
Swaziland	-100	80-85
Syria	150	70-75
Tanganyika	50	90-95
Thailand	75	45-50
Togoland (Fr.)	-100	90-95
Tunisia	120	80-85
Uganda	85	70-75
Union of South Africa	400	55-60
Venezuela	640	45-50
Viet-Nam	-100	80-85
Yemen	-100	95-99
Zanzibar	110	90-95

[1] Figures are based on a 1955-57 average and were taken from a list published by the Statistical Office of the United Nations in Dec., 1958, except where I was able to get on-the-spot data which seemed more specific.

[2] Figures are as of 1950 and were obtained from *World Illiteracy at Mid-Century*, published by UNESCO in 1957. These were used because of consistency; figures for later years are fragmentary when available at all, and put together by different organizations with different standards, and therefore did not seem to me as useful; but it should be borne in mind that in countries such as Indonesia and the Belgian Congo much work has recently been done.

This table shows clearly that in most of the Hungry World democracy is not enough. Limited and temporary authoritarianism is a necessity. How can it be kept limited and temporary? Through what policies and attitudes can the United States and indeed the developed nations of the world help our nascent neighbors solve their problems? These questions I shall attempt to answer in the last chapter.

But first I want to examine the way in which the Communist countries are dealing with their problems.

Five ⬤ *The Communist Challenge*

On August 15, 1958, fresh from several months in Africa, I stepped into a TU-104A at the Prague airport for my first visit to the Soviet Union in seventeen years. The twin-engine transport plane, actually a redesigned Bison bomber, climbed to thirty-three thousand feet in twenty-two minutes and swept off to Moscow at 610 miles an hour. This plane was one of some sixty operated by Aeroflot and several satellite air lines nearly two years before the United States began using jets for scheduled passenger service.

Twenty-five minutes after landing I had cleared customs, immigration, and health and was driving into Moscow past apartment-studded suburbs in what ten years previously had been empty fields.

In two weeks in Moscow, Leningrad, and Riga I met and talked with more than a score of old friends and as many new ones about everything from Hungary and concentration camps to modern art and economic aid. Not a single Soviet friend who was in town during my visit refused to see me.

On my second evening in Moscow I was invited to a party attended by a score of Soviet men and women of many occupations. Two episodes were symbolic of the changes that have recently occurred in the U.S.S.R.

121

I was introduced to a young woman named Yasenskaya. I was struck by the name, for I recalled that Bruno Yasenski was one of the most promising young writers in the Soviet Union in the early 1930's when I worked in that country. In 1936 he had disappeared; in 1937, as we later learned, he had been shot for alleged espionage. His wife was arrested. Their daughter, then a child, was taken from her mother and raised in an institution. After Stalin's death the Soviet government conferred on Bruno Yasenski the posthumous rehabilitation which, though no comfort to him, brought freedom to his wife after twenty years of confinement. In the light of this background, I was fascinated to learn that the young woman was indeed the daughter, now working in Moscow.

This was particularly interesting in the context of the contemporary altercation surrounding the life and work of Poet Boris Pasternak. The inconveniences suffered by Pasternak during 1958 are well known. But Boris Pasternak is still alive and writing. Had he written *Dr. Zhivago* twenty years earlier he would probably have been shot. His voice would have been strangled in some cellar as was Bruno Yasenski's, and the world might later have learned what had happened to him.

It would be silly in the light of Pasternak's experiences to speak of any real freedom of literary expression in the U.S.S.R. It would be unwise, on the other hand, to overlook the difference between the way Pasternak was treated in the 1950's and the fate of Yasenski in the 1930's, namely, the difference between being alive and being dead.

There is a moral here: the Soviet Union today is still a tyrannical dictatorship. But it is less tyrannical and less dictatorial than it was some years ago.

A second episode occurred at this Moscow party. I was talking with three Russians. One was a Communist party member, an upper middle-level functionary in the party organization. Another was a doctor, and the third was a journalist. I told them of my visit to Bhilai, where Soviet technicians are helping the

Indians build a steel mill—a $110-million job, the biggest single piece of foreign aid the Soviet government has undertaken. A vigorous argument developed as the party member defended Soviet foreign aid, while the other two criticized it, using phrases which sounded like the Chicago *Tribune*.

This was an interesting discussion because it was carried out in front of a foreigner in a country where twenty years ago no such remarks would have been made. In the thirties there were some ten or fifteen million Soviet citizens constantly in concentration camps, unpleasant places where the average life expectancy was somewhat shorter than the average sentence and everyone knew it, and it deterred people from discussing controversial issues. Today such discussions are commonplace.

MORE FOOD

These increases in freedom in the Soviet Union have resulted from a significant improvement in material welfare of the people during the past several years. The basic human desires for food, clothing, and shelter have today been fairly well satisfied for most of the people in the Soviet Union. Food is adequate, though frequently not tasty. A physician friend of mine told me that Soviet medical literature has begun to deal seriously with the problem of obesity. During the previous forty years the problem did not exist in the Soviet Union because people did not get enough to eat.

The clothing worn by Soviet citizens is not graceful or stylish, but sturdy. In two weeks in three cities in the Soviet Union I saw not one person without shoes.

The housing situation is more difficult, but they at least have reached the point of decency for Soviet conditions, namely, not more than one family per room.

Twenty years ago the unfortunate family was that with no wall, the family whose allotment of floor space was in the middle of a room, surrounded by other families who had the privacy of a wall. Now the one-family room has become normal, and the multiroom, one-family apartment is beginning to fall within the hopes of the Soviet citizen.

While present living standards in the Soviet Union seem low to Westerners, again and again I heard Russians say: "We have never had it so good. And if there is no war, we are confident that life will get even better."

As material standards improved, the Soviet citizen began to interest himself in the area of freedom. He started to ask questions: Why does the Soviet government jam radio broadcasts from abroad? Why can't we travel abroad on vacation? Why does the Soviet press withhold certain information from us? These implied demands for more freedom placed the Soviet government in a difficult position. It had to choose between going back and readopting those punitive, administrative measures which characterized the purges of the 1930's or else give way gradually to these demands.

MORE FREEDOM

I believe that the Soviet government decided to do the latter not because of any new-found respect for freedom, but, rather, because it realized that going back now to purging might jeopardize the very existence of the Soviet power at the hands of a popular insurrection. So, bit by bit, the government is making concessions to what is becoming Soviet public opinion.

In Brussels in August I saw two or three hundred Soviet tourists traveling. In Moscow I went to three different churches —a Russian Orthodox, a Roman Catholic, and a Baptist. All of them were full—men and women, young and old, officers in uniform. The churches are still harassed by numerous restrictions, but they are freer than they were.

In my profession, journalism, if one takes no news as zero and all the news as 100, I believe that whereas twenty years ago perhaps the official media in the Soviet Union gave the Soviet citizens forty, now it may be sixty-five; when it reaches eighty or so (and it is increasing), I believe the Soviet Union will stop radio jamming, further broadening freedom in another area.

Thus two things are simultaneously going on in the Soviet Union: material conditions are improving, and freedoms are becoming more available to the Soviet citizenry.

TWO PER CENT PER YEAR

I tried to find some arithmetical expression for these two parallel developments. I talked in this interest with friends—planners, economists, journalists, writers—and came up with this rough picture: the gross national product of the U.S.S.R. is increasing by about 8 per cent a year. The population-increase coefficient is about 2 per cent a year. The planners are consciously trying to bring about an annual per capita increase in consumption of about 2 per cent a year. Parenthetically, this is just about the gradient at which United States per capita consumption has been increasing over the past several decades. The Soviet government thus maintains for itself a cushion of some 4 per cent of its GNP, which it can use on revolutions in Guatemala, steel mills in India, volunteers in Iraq, or other projects that it considers of importance.

I hesitate to apply percentages to freedom, but I think that something of the same nature is going on in this area. The Soviet government is trying to increase substantively every year the degree of freedom its citizens enjoy, confident that so much freedom has been withheld from them for so long that this can continue for many years without seriously jeopardizing the control of the Soviet economy by the party and government.

SLICING THE PIE

One question plagued me constantly in the Soviet Union. How can so many people work as hard as they work in a country as big and as rich as the Soviet Union is and still remain so poor in absolute terms? Here again I consulted my economist friends and examined the fragmentary and conflicting statistical estimates made by such bodies as the Office of Intelligence Research and Analysis of the United States Department of State. After making corrections for differences in pricing which seemed to me appropriate, I came up with the following, which I submit with confidence of accuracy within a margin of error of 50 per cent.

If one takes the gross national product of the United States and the U.S.S.R. as pies, our pie in 1958 was about three times theirs, about $440 billion, compared to about $140 billion. However, we sliced our pies differently. In the Soviet Union they divided their GNP pie in three roughly equal parts. They consumed one-third, they invested nearly one-third, and they spent one-third on defense and administration. In our country we divided our pie into three very unequal parts. We consumed about two-thirds, we invested about one-sixth, and we spent about one-sixth on defense and administration. Thus the United States consumed twice as large a slice of a pie three times bigger for a population one-third smaller.

Put in terms of passenger automobiles, we now have 56,000,-000 of them to the Soviet Union's 700,000. The average Soviet citizen goes through life without getting into a passenger automobile.

Nor will this situation soon change. The Seven Year Plan promulgated with such fanfare by Nikita Khrushchev in 1958 provides for an increase of only 25 per cent in passenger cars. In 1965 production is planned at one-twentieth of our current output.

But bicycles and trucks, radio sets, and houses will be produced in millions. Already in 1958 the Soviet Union turned out four times as many machine tools and graduated three times as many engineers as the United States. This means that in a generation Russians may ride while others, less provident, may walk.

At the same time Khrushchev promised in mid-1958 that direct taxes on Soviet citizens may soon be discontinued. Only economists realize that Soviet government revenue comes almost entirely from indirect "turnover" taxes and from the profits on state-owned industry. For millions of unsophisticates in the Hungry World the measure will be made to look like a huge achievement of socialist planning.

COMPARISONS

My brief visit to Russia in 1958 was most useful to me because I could draw comparisons with the Russia I knew in the 1930's, when I spent five years as an industrial worker in Magnitogorsk amid the heroism and hunger of the first Five Year Plan. I watched illiterate Bashkirs herded into barracks along with dispossessed Kulaks for forced labor under conditions far more brutal than those of African mine workers I saw in 1958. I saw some die of hunger and cold and typhus. I knew that others were shot for protesting or attempting to escape.

For in those days, only a generation ago, Russia was part of the Hungry World. It was in many respects where Asia and Africa are today. Immense and impenetrable, its cold as oppressive as tropical heat, Russia wallowed in misery and backwardness century after century until a combination of outside pressures and domestic stupidities destroyed the fabric of the old society, leaving a hungry people to fall under the domination of a small group of ruthless and determined men ablaze with an ideology. Asia and Africa, more vast and even more backward, are now going through a similar process. They desperately need a generation of belt-tightening and hard work to start developing their economies. But so far neither an indigenous leadership group nor an indigenous ideology has appeared to fill the vacuum left by dissolving colonialism. The Hungry World knows only its new desires—more food, clothes, bicycles, radios, guns, and also freedom, dignity, and universal suffrage. And to these hungry people today the voice of Moscow speaks with experience, confidence, and sympathy.

THE SOVIET PACKAGE

In only forty years, the Soviet leaders say, Russia has transformed not only her economy but her culture by purposeful planning under a small group of leaders who know where they are going. "Africans and Asians, you can do the same thing." And the Africans and Asians find much of interest as they begin to study the Soviet economy and its accomplishments.

Historically, high capital formation rates in underdeveloped countries were forced by making people work long hours for bare subsistence (slavery). But in the Hungry World of today this cannot be done. It is the wrong century. Even in backward Ethiopia there is an eight-hour day. Everywhere the masses are demanding and getting not only higher wages but a broadened franchise. It is politically impossible today to force disenfranchised masses to work hard for low wages—as the Afrikaners, I fear, will shortly discover.

However, the Communists have worked out a system for maintaining high capital formation rates in underdeveloped areas. With the aid of a Communist party which permeates every facet of a country's life, they *get* people to work hard. They persuade the masses that they are working for themselves. Their captive trade unions suggest lower wages and higher norms. They make a cult of industrialization. Blast furnaces become images of progress and aspiration. The hydroelectric plant, the bridge, the railroad become the symbols of power stamped into the minds of youth with every instrument of the propaganda orchestra.

Such "socially useless" industries as cosmetics manufacturing and advertising virtually cease to exist. The effort of the whole community is concentrated on industrialization *now*, in order to achieve some distant and nebulous nirvana. Any citizen selfish or foolish enough to demand butter rather than turbines, more wages for less work, is accused of opportunism, subversion, treason, and heresy—and frequently executed after a groveling confession, thereby furnishing the simple people with devil images to contrast with the labor-hero-god images.

And the Soviet Union itself has demonstrated that this Communist system *works*. During the 1930's the U.S.S.R. pushed its capital formation rate up near 50 per cent without outside investments; and today, with considerably relaxed conditions and more consumer goods, capital formation is still running in the neighborhood of 30 per cent. In Soviet Central Asia and other parts of Moscow's vast internal colonial empire, development was spectacular, as skilled personnel and machinery were brought in from European Russia to help local manpower develop local resources for the "people."

Of course there were unpleasantnesses which jarred the citizens of the Hungry World as they examined Soviet achievements at home, the concentration camp, the torture chamber, the censored press, the regimented school. But for most Asians and Africans human suffering seems as immutable as the weather; and besides, if there was talk of torture and censorship, both were to be found close at home, in Algiers, Ciudad Trujillo, Pusan, and Baghdad.

Let me try in one paragraph to summarize the challenge presented by Soviet performance at home to the Hungry World.

One major test of the effectiveness of any government or system of government is: What can it get its people to do? During the past forty years the Soviet government has been able to cajole, browbeat, torture, persuade, and inspire its people to produce much while consuming little. The difference between these magnitudes has been channeled, for the most part, into two massive efforts: first, the modernization and industrialization of what a generation ago was a backward economy; second, an impressive school system, which has taught more than 100 million adults to read and write and graduated some eight million young people from institutions of higher education, which, particularly in technology, maintain high standards.

These things the Soviet Union has done at immense cost in

human life and suffering, both those caused by two great wars and those imposed by an arbitrary and ruthless government. But today the Soviet Union is able to give its citizens a little more to eat and a little more freedom than they had last year. In addition, the economy is producing enough surpluses to launch a major program of economic aid and political activity directed at the Hungry World.

Ruble Diplomacy

From its birth on through World War II the Soviet Union has been on the defensive abroad. It fought at first to free itself from foreign armies, for geographic and economic survival, then for recognition. The revolutionary dynamism with which Leon Trotsky was associated was subordinated for a generation to Stalin's drive for socialism in one country.

During these years the initiative was in other hands, and the Soviet leaders often lost such tenuous offensive gambits as they tried, like that in Spain, and were repeatedly forced to retreat before great-power pressure, as they did in selling the Chinese Eastern Railroad to Japan in 1935.

During this period Soviet influence in the underdeveloped countries was minimal. Moscow had virtually no contact with Africa, Latin America, or the Middle East, while its influence in Asia was limited to Soviet Central Asia and China, where communism was contained and harassed for a generation by Chiang Kai-shek and the Kuomintang.

What the Soviet government did do, however, during those difficult years was to prepare cadres for the future. As early as 1921 the University of the Toilers of the East in Leningrad began to teach Oriental languages, history, and economics to young and trustworthy Soviet citizens, while several thousand carefully selected Communists from all over the world were brought to Moscow for training in the famed Lenin School or other specialized institutions. Such men as Ho Chi-minh, along with others perhaps still to be heard from in the Middle East and Africa, were given expert training in everything from guerrilla warfare to parliamentary procedure.

World War II weakened the Soviet economy, but at its termination Soviet armies controlled Eastern and Central Europe and Manchuria. In an understandable but unpopular attempt to assuage the crying needs of the Soviet Union itself, the first five years or so after the war were used in massive organized Soviet looting from the Rhine to the Yellow Sea, while Stalin's friends and agents sought to spread Communist control by conspiracy and military force in both Europe and Asia. The last major success in this effort in Europe came in 1947 in Czechoslovakia. Then after the partial loss of Yugoslavia the front stabilized as Western Europe regained economic health and strength.

In Asia the Chinese Communist victory in 1949 inspired both jubilation and apprehension from Minsk to Saigon. For some months it seemed to many that communism might sweep the Orient. But after the sobering Korean war and the partition of Indochina, a power balance seemed to have been achieved.

By that time Stalin's death and the political independence achieved in most of Asia and the Middle East had changed the political and economic picture radically, while new weapons had made large-scale warfare an increasingly unpromising instrument for the solution of any international problems.

Stalin's successors set about the job of winning the world for communism by economic and political means. In doing this they have been able to draw on the increasing strength of the Soviet economy and the stature and prestige the U.S.S.R. acquired during the war.

Moscow leaders have planned the job in a professional fashion, as an American manufacturer plans the acquisition of a new market or a general staff lays out a campaign. At every step costs have been balanced against resources and results;

every field of human activity has been regarded as a battlefield
for the deployment of opposing forces.

THE DIPLOMATIC OFFENSIVE

Diplomatic and trade relations have been established with a
number of countries with whom Moscow had no previous con-
tact. Since the war the Soviet Union has opened diplomatic
and/or trade relations with Argentina, Bolivia, Brazil, Burma,
Cambodia, Ceylon, Chile, Costa Rica, the Dominican Republic,
Ecuador, Egypt, El Salvador, East and West Germany, Ghana,
Guatemala, Guinea, Haiti, India, Indonesia, Israel, Japan, Laos,
Lebanon, Liberia, Libya, Morocco, Nepal, New Zealand,
Nicaragua, Pakistan, San Marino, Saudi Arabia, Sudan, Switzerland, Syria, Thailand, Tunisia, and the United Arab Republic.
In the case of some of these countries relations were established,
but representatives were never actually exchanged. But in most
instances embassies and consulates, frequently in great force,
made their appearance in parts of the world where previously
Russia had had no contacts.

Invariably these missions were staffed by Soviet citizens well
acquainted with even the most obscure languages. Where did
they come from? Some were old-timers. But most were the
products of the impressive attempts made by the Soviet Union
at home after the war to teach a large picked group of Soviet
citizens exotic languages and the history and mores of distant
lands and peoples.

PERSONNEL TRAINING

One of the most impressive of these attempts is the current
"experimental program" in Soviet primary and secondary
schools. In Moscow Boarding School Number 23, for example,
150 students are currently starting at the second-grade level
(eight years old) to study either Hindi or Urdu. In two boarding
schools in Leningrad, Chinese and Hindi are taught beginning
at the second grade. In Tashkent five secondary schools teach

one or more of the following languages: Hindi, Urdu, Chinese, and Arabic. In Stalinbad and Baku several secondary schools teach Persian and Arabic. Other secondary schools in half a dozen other Soviet central Asian cities teach Persian, Urdu, Arabic, and Kurdish.

On the university level languages are taught in the context of area studies, which include history, economics, culture, and sociology. In both Moscow and Leningrad such programs are available on China, India, Arabia, Indonesia, Japan, Turkey, Viet-Nam, Korea. These courses of study in Moscow are now scheduled to last six years, and forty students were enrolled during the first two years.

Specialists in the African countries and languages were scheduled to start in Leningrad in 1957, in Moscow in 1958, and in Tashkent in 1959.

In addition to these, two-year courses for area specialists and six-month refresher courses are open to adults designated by their ministries, where presumably they already occupy responsible positions.

Several ministries run their own special area schools. The Institute of International Relations in Moscow, run by the Ministry of Foreign Affairs, is a sort of foreign policy West Point and has a current enrollment of about one thousand regular students and 500 extension students. Some 300 of the former are specialists in exotic languages. It is known that the Soviet security authorities have their own area and language schools, but I was unable to learn any details.

Research in exotic areas is concentrated in the Institute of Eastern Studies of the Academy of Sciences, with branches in Moscow and Leningrad. Branches are soon to be established in half a dozen other cities in the U.S.S.R.

Thus when I met half a dozen Russians at a diplomatic party in Karachi, all fluent in Urdu, while not a single American in the United States Embassy there was able to use the language effectively, it was not an accident, but the result of a serious and still rapidly expanding Soviet program of studies which is getting high priorities and able students.

Nor are Soviet educational institutions neglecting mundane languages like English. In late 1958 I was invited to address a convocation at the University of Minnesota along with another speaker, who turned out to be an attaché of the Soviet Embassy in Washington, a thin, sandy-haired, freckle-faced man of about thirty, who got up in front of some 1,500 students and professors and made an excellent forty-five-minute speech on Soviet education in slightly accented but grammatical and idiomatic English. He was factual, interesting, showed humor and taste. He avoided politics except when asked specific political questions, when he gave straight party-line answers.

Some weeks later I was lunching with William S. B. Lacy of the United States State Department, who negotiated our cultural exchange agreement with the U.S.S.R. I told him of this experience and asked whether we had anyone in Moscow doing the same kind of job. We did not, I was told, partly because no invitations had come in for such speaking engagements, but also because we had as yet few, if any, Americans qualified to do the job.

Having trained personnel and established contact with the Hungry World through local Communist parties and Soviet diplomatic missions, the Russians made surveys and studies, country plans and position papers. Then they divided the campaign along geographic and functional lines. A primary area of activity was in trade.

TRADE BEFORE AID

Soviet foreign trade, still less than 4 per cent of world trade, was expanded during the post-Stalin years thanks to major Moscow efforts, including an international advertising campaign channeled largely through trade fairs.

Sensibly desirous of making virtues out of their liabilities, Soviet trade experts have sought to use the immense demand for goods in the Soviet bloc as an asset by "taking surpluses off the hands of" overstocked nations on the other side of the curtain. Moscow has condescended in this way to buy cotton from Egypt, rice from Burma, tea and rubber from Ceylon; the Russians have dangled cotton orders under the twitching noses of Pakistan officials and bought significant quantities of sugar from Cuba and animal products from Argentina and Uruguay. In every instance these commodities have been in oversupply, and in many cases the United States has been giving away its own surpluses to the chagrin of other producers. The Russians thus have hoped to convert the twin United States virtues of productivity and generosity into political liabilities, and in some cases they succeeded.

The Soviet Union has paid for these purchases in manufactured goods, including arms produced by the famed Czech Skoda works. Soviet industrial equipment, for example, has gone to China in return for rice and pork, which the Chinese have snatched from the mouths of their own consumers. The Russians have often re-exported these commodities to third countries outside the bloc.

In every case astute officials in Moscow in monopoly control of all imports and exports not only for the U.S.S.R. but for the entire bloc have used foreign trade as an instrument of political infiltration and influence. They could juggle prices and priorities as they chose. When the West responded with restrictions such as those embodied in the Battle Act, Moscow beat the radio waves with indignant demands for freedom of trade, which of course meant freedom for Soviet monopolies to run rings around the West's competitive buyers and sellers.

By 1957 Soviet officials were able to undertake some irritating experiments in economic warfare which caused wide comment. They dumped on the world market large quantities both of tin and aluminum, apparently to see what the effects would be on prices and on the blood pressure of "Wall Street imperialists."

Sometimes the Russians have outsmarted themselves. Having made friends in Cairo by buying more than half of Egypt's

cotton crop, they have angered their new friends by reselling
some of it to Egypt's normal customers. The shameless use of
trade pressures to bring down Finland's government in 1958
boomeranged, as the Russians belatedly realized that they had
thrown a brick through their own show window, and Khrushchev
himself trundled up to Leningrad to patch things up with Russia's tough northern neighbors. The most spectacular blooper
was the deal under which thousands of tons of Soviet cement
arrived in Burma on the eve of the monsoon and spoiled on the
docks, while the Burmese rice that had paid for it was shipped
to the Philippines for hard currency the Burmese desperately
needed.

Indications are that the Russians now realize how much
damage they can do themselves with such sharp dealing and that
they will try to avoid it in the future.

But in any case, the Russians plan to continue wherever possible using foreign trade rather than foreign aid in pursuing
their policies in the Hungry World, and their growing ability
to buy the materials and primary crops from the underdeveloped countries and pay in needed manufactured goods and
technical aid will constitute an increasing challenge.

GOLD STANDARD

For several years some bankers in the West have been apprehensive about Moscow's intention to use its allegedly huge gold
reserves to upset Western currencies. Soviet academician K. B.
Ostrovityanov's recent statement, to the effect that, as the Soviet
Union completes its Seven Year Plan and overtakes the United
States in per capita production of important commodities, the
ruble will replace the dollar as the medium of world trade, has
sharpened these anxieties, although at present the ruble is not
even strong enough to circulate freely within the Soviet bloc,
and its export to the West is strictly forbidden by the Soviet
government.

In 1958 in Johannesburg and in Zurich, and in Moscow in

1958 and 1959, I looked into these stories as best I could, and, after comparing notes with other students, I concluded to my own satisfaction that estimates of Soviet production and reserves of gold have been exaggerated. I put the former figure at about 280 million dollars a year, the latter at not more than three billion dollars. It is definitely known that Soviet sales of gold in London and Switzerland during recent years have been as follows, in millions of dollars per year: 1955—70; 1956—150; 1957—262 (paying for Hungary); 1958—210; 1959—(April only) 23. I believe that the Soviet Union can continue mining and selling gold at roughly the current rate indefinitely, leaving perhaps a few million dollars a year for subversive activities abroad, and using the proceeds of sales to make up trade deficits. If necessary the Soviet Union can cut its reserves to near zero, as the ruble's stability at home depends on the power of the Soviet government rather than on gold backing, and the ruble has no international position to require gold support.

I must point out that some other students of Soviet economics have opinions quite different from mine. But I am convinced that it is not Soviet gold, but the fact that the Soviet government has achieved domestic price stability without using gold, while the "valuta ruble," a purely imaginary unit of value, serves quite effectively in intra-bloc trade, again without gold backing, that challenges our monetary theories and practices in the eyes of the Hungry World.

ECONOMIC AID

To supplement its trade offensive and to accommodate those nations without exportable surpluses, the Soviet government inaugurated an economic aid program in 1953. The first move was a Soviet announcement that the U.S.S.R. would contribute four million rubles to the United Nations technical aid program, previously condemned as a tool of imperialism. From 1953 to 1957 the Soviet Union launched a massive economic aid program in underdeveloped countries. More than 80 per

cent of the aid came from the Soviet Union itself, the rest
ostensibly originated in Czechoslovakia, East Germany, China,
and other bloc countries.

The principal recipients of this aid were six countries: Yugoslavia, India, Egypt, Syria, Afghanistan, and Indonesia. During
the four years nearly $1.6 billion was spent. In 1958 the Soviet
government undertook an additional one billion dollars of aid
to eighteen underdeveloped countries. More than two-thirds of
this sum was for economic as opposed to military aid.

The following table gives a summary picture:

*Estimated Value of Soviet Bloc Nonmilitary Credit Agreements
Signed with Underdeveloped Countries**

1953 to 1957

Lender	Million U.S. Dollars	Per Cent	Recipient	Million U.S. Dollars	Per Cent (Inc. Yugo-slavia)
U.S.S.R.	1,227	78	Yugoslavia	444	28
Other bloc	354	22	India	362	23
Czechoslovakia	176	11	Egypt	213	14
East Germany	103	6	Syria	184	12
China	58	4	Afghanistan	115	7
Hungary	7	1	Indonesia	113	7
Poland	7	1	Ceylon	26	
Rumania	3	1	Cambodia	22	
Total	1,581	100	Burma	22	
			Turkey	22	
			Argentina	21	
			Paraguay	15	
			Nepal	13	
			Sudan	5	
			Lebanon	2	
			Yemen	2	
			Total	1,581	100

* Taken from "Soviet Economic Aid" by Joseph Berliner, Council on
Foreign Relations, 1958.

The largest single recipient of Soviet foreign aid is Yugoslavia, formerly in the bloc.* In nearly every case the Soviet foreign economic aid has been expressed in loans or credits at low rates of interest rather than in grants. When gifts are offered, they are usually of a quasi-personal nature as when Khrushchev gave an airplane to Nehru and a hospital to Burma. This is, I was told in Moscow, a matter of policy on the part of the Soviet authorities, who believe that aid in the form of long-term, low-interest loans is most compatible with dignity on the part of the recipient. In this connection I learned in Moscow that before they launched their own aid programs, Soviet planners studied carefully American programs already in operation and noted that gifts often caused hostility and animosity instead of gratitude.

Soviet aid usually has had few visible strings attached. Far less information was required to formulate Soviet loans than was demanded by American authorities, and often Soviet aid was in large identifiable projects like the paved streets in Kabul or the Bhilai steel mill rather than buried deep in anonymous pumppriming activities like most of United States economic aid. The reason for this difference is that the purpose of Soviet economic aid is frankly propagandistic and political. The purpose of United States economic aid is to strengthen the economy of the recipient rather than to make friends for the United States.

TECHNICAL ASSISTANCE

In addition to loans and credits for development, the Soviet bloc has begun a widely dispersed program of technical assistance. During the past two years industrial and scientific aid has been given by the U.S.S.R. to a score of countries from Indonesia to Paraguay. Among other projects the Soviet Union is now training Egyptian physicists who will staff a thermo-

* Since early 1959 Soviet aid to Yugoslavia has been suspended.

nuclear reactor which the Soviet Union is building in Cairo for the Egyptians.

In maximizing technical assistance, the Soviet Union is wisely capitalizing on the success of Soviet technical higher schools by exporting technological brainpower. It costs the Soviet economy less to educate an engineer, give him some experience, and then maintain him abroad than it does the United States, if only because the Soviet technician is paid so much less and has not yet learned to expect or demand the expensive and often politically embarrassing luxuries required to tempt American technicians to far countries.

MILITARY ASSISTANCE

Soviet military assistance outside the bloc has been limited to Egypt, Indonesia, Yemen, Syria, and Iraq. The total so far made available to these countries is about half a billion dollars and in every case was in the form of loans to purchase Soviet and Czech military equipment.

INTRAMURAL SOVIET BLOC AID

Soviet aid within the bloc has been extensive, and information on it has been fragmentary and often contradictory. Khrushchev stated in 1956 that since the war the U.S.S.R. had granted a total of twenty-one billion rubles on long-term credits and loans to the "people's democracies." During the two years after the 20th Party Congress the Soviet Union extended a total of some two billion dollars in new aid to the bloc countries. It also canceled debts to about the same amount. Many of these debts, however, had been incurred during the period of organized Soviet postwar looting, often expressed through joint companies in which Soviet ownership constituted seized enemy assets. Furthermore, since about 1954, I am sure Soviet profits on intra-bloc trade have been substantially greater than total Soviet aid and credits to these countries.

EVALUATION

When one adds up all the Soviet loans, gifts, and credits as well as military aid and technical assistance, the total comes to something like two and a half billion dollars annually, substantially less than the five billion or so the United States has been giving.

In absolute terms Soviet aid to the Hungry World is indeed great—and it is growing. The real challenge, however, is that Soviet economic aid programs present the Hungry World with an alternative and an opportunity to bargain and compare.

Asians and Africans are beginning to remark that the Soviet Union does not "invest" capital in the traditional way, that Soviet technical and administrative personnel active in the Hungry World tend to be unostentatious and effective and frequently know local languages and live on standards comparable to those of the local people. Most important, perhaps, they remark that the Soviet Union does not ask or take concessions. Moscow deals with governments, and the enterprises and assets built become the property of the recipient nation.

The Soviet Union has demonstratively refused any association with the West in rendering aid to the Hungry World because it regards all United States aid in this area as being part of a rapacious search for profits plus an attempt to get rid of surpluses on which "Wall Street monopolists have made millions."

That this apparent Soviet unselfishness is illusory is easy to demonstrate in terms of specific examples in many areas where the Soviet Union has used aid to exert direct political influence as it did in Syria, in Yugoslavia, and in Egypt.*

* For anyone interested in more details on Soviet economic aid, its chemistry and effects, I can recommend highly *Soviet Economic Aid* by Joseph Berliner, a readable, authoritative, and balanced treatment of the entire subject.

BHILAI

I had an opportunity in 1957 to visit the Bhilai steel mill and to talk with the Indian and the Soviet engineers and officials working there. I even found several engineers who had worked in Magnitogorsk at the same time I did, twenty-five years ago. I wandered freely over an immense field spread with the machinery and equipment sent from the Soviet Union and watched some ninety Soviet technicians, living quietly with their families in the same kind of modest housing that the Indian technicians occupied and working co-operatively with the Indians on the job. I was impressed by the fact that many of the Soviet engineers were top men, and that the whole job was under the supervision of a deputy minister, until he was killed in a hunting accident.

I found a high degree of co-operation among the technical staff and a very great public recognition on the part of the Indians that they were getting a fine steel mill from the Soviet Union. Most lower-level Indians did not seem to realize that they were going to have to pay the Soviet Union back for the mill along with some thirty million dollars in interest. I talked with some Indians who refused to believe me when I told them that Russia was charging interest, so effective is the propaganda utilization the Russians made of their aid programs.

EGYPT

I have also seen some of the results of Soviet economic and military aid in Egypt. There the nearly half a billion dollars of Soviet aid has been accompanied by Soviet planners and technicians on several levels, including ministerial advisers who sit in Cairo and help with the formulation and execution of policy. These men, plus the fact that the Soviet bloc was buying Egyptian cotton no one else seemed to want and paying in arms that others were unwilling to provide, went far toward bringing

Egypt under Soviet political influence, until the events in 1958 in Iraq began pushing Egypt back toward the West.

Educational, Cultural, and Information Activities

Often cultural and educational activities can be even more important than economic aid in influencing political developments and policies.

The Russian hospital in Addis Ababa, for example, which I had a chance to visit in 1958, was established three generations ago by the czarist government and is now staffed by Soviet administrators and medical professionals. It is an immensely effective projection of the Soviet image into a continent so far but little penetrated by the Soviet Union. Another more recently established Soviet hospital in Teheran which I visited in 1957 is trying to do a similar job against heavier odds. In 1958 the Soviet Union began the construction of a 500-bed hospital in Phnom Penh, and thousands of tons of Soviet building materials arrived on the site, which I watched being prepared in 1957 with equipment furnished under American economic aid. Libya has accepted Soviet offers to build, equip, and staff two hospitals in that country. Other Soviet hospitals are being built in Nepal and Burma.

In 1958 the Soviet government began an intensive program of scholarships for advanced students from the underdeveloped countries to study in the field of medicine and public health in various institutions in the U.S.S.R. Students have already come from Bolivia, Nepal, Indonesia, Egypt, and a number of African countries.

Moscow has also been quick to engage in spectacular emergency aid. In 1958, for example, when cholera threatened parts of Indonesia, the Soviet Union flew in a special plane with 500 liters of cholera vaccine to Jakarta. A little later ten Soviet planes and forty-five pilots were sent to Iran to spray a whole province threatened with a locust invasion.

In the literary field the Soviet government has been most active. In the first place, Soviet books, often English or French classics having no direct political content, have been sold in many parts of the Hungry World at prices well below those at which any local or Western publisher could sell them. I have seen such books in large quantities for sale in India, Egypt, Indonesia, Ceylon, North Africa, and many parts of Europe.

Soviet press attachés in many capitals are effective in supplying local editors with releases and other material. They also frequently spend money judiciously and effectively. In Damascus several years ago I chanced on a Syrian editor who told me he was getting $100 a month from the Soviet Embassy as "friendship money." In a country like Syria, where large numbers of newspapers fight hard for limited circulations, a small cash subsidy often makes the difference between solvency and bankruptcy. I was told at that time that the Soviet Embassy was subsidizing about sixteen Syrian newspapers. In Karachi the following year, while officials of the American and British embassies tended to fuss over the cosmopolitan English language press, I found the Soviet Information people diligently cultivating the up-country Urdu weeklies.

Several times during the past four years the Soviet Union has put on major conferences for Asian and African writers. One on the biggest was in Tashkent in October 1958, which was attended by some two hundred writers from thirty-nine states, including Burma, Japan, Ceylon, Cambodia, the Philippines, Afghanistan, Thailand, Turkey, Pakistan, Egypt, Algeria, Madagascar, and a dozen African dependencies. The proceedings were carried on in Chinese, Arabic, French, English, and Russian with simultaneous translations.

Much has been written about the activities of the Soviet radio in broadcasting in all directions. It outshouts the BBC and the Voice of America in most parts of the Hungry World. The recently begun broadcasts in Quechua, for example, for the plateau Indians in Bolivia and Peru is indicative of Radio

Moscow's specialization and diligence. But less has been written about such projects as the youth festivals held every two years in various parts of the world. One of the most spectacular was that produced in Moscow in August 1957. It attracted some thirty-five thousand young people from all over the world and was for most of them an unforgettable experience. Some of the roughly $200 million spent on this festival came from a special bond issue bought by Soviet citizens. The project cost substantially more than the total annual budget of the United States Information Agency.

The ability and willingness of the Soviet government to spend this kind of money merchandising communism for the Hungry World is in itself a measure of the challenge it presents.

CHINA

The latest, and in the long run, most important expression of the Communist challenge comes from China.

When the Chinese Communists won their long civil war in 1949 and pushed the Nationalists from the mainland, striking similarities existed between China and India. Both had per capita incomes of about forty-five dollars a year, both were producing less than two million tons of steel, both were predominantly agricultural and largely locally self-sufficient. Both had tens of millions of urban and rural unemployed or underemployed. Both had strong traditions of individualism and stoicism. There were differences, of course. China was nearly twice as large in population; India had better roads and a far better civil service. India had almost escaped the war damage so vast in China.

But both faced the necessity of working hard, of saving and investing, if mass starvation was to be avoided. The race between these two countries has been a classic, watched carefully by millions all over the world.

I have tried to watch it. But like many others I have had trouble. For a decade Americans have been forbidden by

United States Government restrictions from traveling to mainland China. I personally believe these travel restrictions are unnecessary and stupid. I know they have been ineffective, as dozens of Americans selected by the Chinese have gone anyhow without State Department permission. I am in the process as I write these lines of trying to arrange to visit China. I hope I succeed. In the meantime, I am able at this point to say only a word about that key country as seen from outside, from Moscow, Hong Kong, and Singapore, from London and New York.

There is a surprising degree of agreement among Communist China's friends and enemies on several points. First and most fundamental is China's population—more than 600,-000,000 and increasing by about thirteen million a year. Since the Communists gained power, the population of the country has grown by more than 100,000,000. A birth-control campaign begun in 1956 has been abandoned in what seems to have been an ominous decision to prepare to survive a possible thermonuclear war.

Nearly everyone agrees that during the past ten years much economic progress has been made in spite of blockade, the Korean War, and lack of any substantial outside credits. On the other side of the ledger, there is no doubt that millions died in the land reform and in punitive measures taken against "capitalists and landlords."

To be more specific, it seems likely that China has increased its steel production to more than ten million tons, outrunning India by about 100 per cent; by intensive agriculture and by building dams and canals to bring new land under the plow, the Chinese have increased agricultural production by perhaps 100 per cent. The new bridge over the Yangtze, completed in 1957, is symbolic of a number of improvements in the transportation network. The entire area of mainland China plus Tibet has been brought for the first time in recent history under the direct administration of a central government. War lords and secret societies have disappeared along with rural money lenders, organized vice, and narcotics trade. Petty corruption has been seriously reduced. Popular campaigns like those against flies, rats, and sparrows have enlisted almost universal co-operation and been spectacularly successful.

These things have been achieved in part by the massive use of forced labor and the almost universal use of "volunteers."

The capital for these many developments has come largely from the Chinese people either through confiscation, taxation, or "voluntary contribution" of everything from money and real property to the pots and pans melted down after their former owners "joined" communes with communal kitchens.

CHINESE-RUSSIAN COMPETITION

In all these enterprises China has been heavily dependent on the U.S.S.R., which has furnished the equipment for some 210 industrial plants and thousands of technicians. But for these favors and for the Soviet military aid received during the Korean War, China is paying through the nose. Eighty per cent of China's exports go to the Soviet bloc. These include the soy beans, pork, bristles, mica, manganese, tung oil, and silks which used to go to the West.

In seeking parallels between the economic development of China and the Soviet Union, the following analogies suggest themselves. In China the period of 1949-1952, the period of reconstruction, corresponded to a whole decade, 1917-1928, in the Soviet Union. The first Five Year Plan in China, 1953-1957, corresponded to Russia's first Five Year Plan, 1928-1932. Both countries got through their first Five Year plans in four years. In the second Five Year Plan China is planning targets proportionally comparable to those of the third Soviet Five Year Plan. In agriculture the Chinese accomplished in their land reform (1949-1952) many of the changes that the Russians achieved only during collectivization—specifically, the liquidation of the kulaks.

In short, the Chinese, starting far lower in industrial power and per capita income than the Russians, have been going

faster. The commune movement in 1958 at first surprised,
then profoundly disturbed the Russians. I found thoughtful
men in Moscow reflecting soberly that China was likely to
cause serious trouble by throwing its huge weight around. This
feeling, I believe, lies behind Khrushchev's insistence on a
summit meeting and a bilateral straightening of accounts with
the United States.

For China has today already become a competitor of the
U.S.S.R. During the past two years the Chinese have even
begun to extend their own still modest programs of foreign aid
to Cambodia, Laos, Nepal, Ceylon, North Korea, and North
Viet-Nam.

All of these achievements are fairly well known throughout
the Hungry World and constitute a challenge in the long run
far more serious than that of the Soviet Union because the
Chinese started more recently with less and because they, like
nearly all the other citizens of the Hungry World, have colored
skins.

COMMUNIST PARTIES

In every area the Communist challenge is implemented and
directed by the world's eighty-odd Communist parties.

In the U.S.S.R. and China huge parties, six and twelve million strong respectively, run the country. Intrenched in every
ministry, factory, university, and newspaper, disciplined and
dedicated Communists work diligently to implement party decisions for the ever-expanding power and prestige of the party.

But we are here more concerned with the parties in the
Hungry World. The United States State Department estimates
that on January 1, 1959, nearly two million men and women
were enrolled in Communist parties in the non-Communist
Hungry World. One million of these were in Indonesia; 250,000
in India, in mass parties able to win elections and perhaps, if
allowed to do so, take over their government.

But in dozens of other countries and territories small disciplined parties, often illegal and underground, implement the

Communist challenge by gathering information, recruiting personnel, penetrating or even organizing trade unions and other organizations, publishing newspapers and leaflets, and preparing for insurrection and civil war. Guided and aided by professionals and experts in the Comintern or Cominform, supported with money and arms when needed, these parties constitute a network unique in the world.

Anyone skeptical of the capacity of a tiny group to exert major influence in a large country should recall that a few thousand Bolsheviks under Lenin took power in war-torn Russia in 1917. Or, more recent and pertinent is the frightening efficiency with which an Iraqi Communist party estimated one thousand strong in January 1959 was close to assuming power by midyear.

Only Black Africa has so far not been penetrated by Communist parties, but I would guess that within five years parties will have been organized there, too.

Here is a list, made up by the State Department's Bureau of Intelligence and Research, of the Communist parties of the Hungry World:

Communist Party Membership

Country	Estimated Membership as of January 1959	Remarks
Afghanistan	No overt Communists	Illegal
Algeria	5,000-10,000	Illegal
Angola	Negligible	Illegal
Argentina	70,000-80,000	Legal
Belgian Congo	Negligible	Legal
Bolivia	4,000	Legal
Brazil	50,000	Illegal
Burma	12,000	Divided into legal parties (largest has app. 5,000 members) and illegal parties (app. 7,000 members)

Country	Estimated Membership as of January 1959	Remarks
Cambodia	1,000 or less	Legal
Cameroons (U.K.)	Negligible	Legal
Ceylon	6,100	4,000 Moscow-oriented
		1,500 Trotskyites
		650 Independent Communists
Chile	20,000-25,000	Legal
China (mainland)	12,720,000	Legal
China (Nationalist)	Believed negligible	Illegal
Colombia	5,000	Legal
Costa Rica	300	Illegal
Ecuador	1,000	Legal
El Salvador	500	Illegal
Ethiopia	Negligible	No CP known to exist
French Equatorial Africa	Negligible	Legal
French West Africa	Negligible	Legal
Gambia	Negligible	No CP known to exist
Ghana	Negligible	No CP known to exist
Guatemala	1,000	Illegal
Honduras	500	Illegal
India	250,000	Legal
Indonesia	1,000,000	Legal
Iran	1,000-2,000	Illegal
Iraq	1,000	Illegal
Israel	2,000	800 of these may be Arabs
Japan	60,000-80,000	Legal
Jordan	250 (3-4,000 active supporters)	Illegal
Kenya	Negligible	No CP known to exist
Korea (South)	Negligible	Illegal
Laos	Probably less than 4,000	Legal
Lebanon	8,000 (Syrian-Lebanese party)	Illegal
Liberia	Negligible	No CP known to exist
Libya	Negligible	No CP known to exist

Country	Estimated Member- ship as of *January 1959*	Remarks
Madagascar	Unknown	Legal
Malaya	5,000	Illegal
Mexico	80,000	Legal
Morocco	1,000-1,500	Illegal
Mozambique	Negligible	Illegal
Nicaragua	200	Illegal
Nigeria	Negligible	No CP known to exist
Pakistan	3,500	Illegal
Panama	Negligible	Illegal
Peru	6,000	Illegal
Philippines	1,000-1,500 includes 500-600 under arms (Huks) and app. 300 Chinese Communists	Illegal
Rhodesias	Negligible	No CP known to exist
Saudi Arabia	Negligible	Illegal
Sierra Leone	Negligible	No CP known to exist
Sudan	750	Illegal
Tanganyika	Negligible	No CP known to exist
Thailand	200 or less Thai CP Up to 5,000 Chinese CP	Legal
Togoland (Fr.)	Negligible	No CP known to exist
Tunisia	250-500	Legal
United Arab Republic	4,000 Egypt 8,000 Syria (Syrian-Lebanese party)	Illegal
Uganda	Negligible	No CP known to exist
Union of South Africa	1,000-2,000	Illegal
Venezuela	30,000-35,000	Legal
Viet-Nam	Unknown (1,500-2,000 estimated infiltration)	Illegal
Yemen	Unknown	No CP known to exist
Zanzibar	Negligible	No CP known to exist

At the heart of communism's challenge, whether transmitted by radio or through party conspiracies, is the appeal to the people of the Hungry World to "fight." For it raises the central question of violence in a world where new weapons have made the use of force extremely dangerous—and where higher conscience and intelligence may soon make its use unnecessary.

The appeal to violence is an expression of the Marxian rejection of humanity and conscience, its assertion that reforms are not granted but seized. Conscience and humanity cannot move men to kindness and generosity in a class society, says the voice of Moscow, because the competitive system makes it mandatory for those with wealth and power to invoke every evil in order to keep and increase both, lest they be outdone by their competitors.

Slavery was abolished, the Communists argue, because of slave revolts and economic pressures. Britain was *forced* to leave India, they say, while today workers can improve their lives only by revolution. The masses of the Hungry World can assure themselves better lives only by rebelling against imperialism. The Florence Nightingales, Leo Tolstoys, and Albert Schweitzers are addled liberals, whose main historic role is to mislead the masses and defend the status quo. So runs the Communist line.

In thus denying the role of the human conscience, the Soviet leaders have, in effect, destroyed it, at least for the time, in their own society. Russian voices of dissent have been strangled silently in the cellars of the Lyubyanka or in the snows of Siberia. In denying man the Soviet leaders share with their less successful ideological cousins, the German Nazis, the opening of the floodgates for the worst in human bestiality—the Katyn massacre (whoever did it), Auschwitz and Vorkuta, the torture chambers of the Gestapo, and the MVD. Both Nazis and Communists prepared the way for such activities by campaigns against humanism and humanity, campaigns still going on today in the Soviet Union. A fairly systematic examination of Soviet school textbooks in 1958 made clear to me, if the daily press left any room for doubt, that the Soviet leaders still believe in struggle and violence as the only way in which basic issues can be settled.

But I must also report that I left Moscow in September 1958 confident that the Russian conscience so magnificently portrayed by Dostoevski and Tolstoy is reasserting itself, in spite of the Soviet government. Indeed, the seeds of a renaissance of conscience are already sprouting. The public debate around Boris Pasternak is encouraging. I found that academic circles in Moscow were aware that famed physicist Peter Kapitsa had spent two years in jail for refusing to work on the H-bomb, and his action won almost universal approval. I found Russians in all walks of life ashamed of their role in Hungary.

These and many other examples convinced me that the Russian conscience is in the process of reasserting itself, bitterly fought by the Soviet oligarchy but likely, within my lifetime, to flower into a new enlightenment after generations of darkness.

Six Partnership in Progress

General Principles

To outline in a few pages an economic, military, and political policy for our relations with the Hungry World would be presumptuous. But I should like to set forth some principles and attitudes which might be useful in formulating detailed policies.

WORLD CO-OPERATION UNDER THE UNITED NATIONS

First and most fundamental, the Hungry World must be fed, or more accurately, it must be helped to learn to feed itself, or chaos and destruction are bound to overtake us all. Even without the cleavages of the cold war, the progressive impoverishment of the already poor would surely move them through envy and desperation to try to seize from us, the affluent few, the wealth we so conspicuously flaunt. And modern technology will soon furnish them cheap and terrible weapons to guarantee that such a conflict would have no victors, and perhaps no survivors.

In this holocaust, if we are improvident enough to allow it to develop, the U.S.S.R. would tend to find itself associated with Canada, Australia, the United States, and parts of Europe

155

as "have" nations trying to defend their favorable ratio of wealth and resources to population against the hungry "have-nots." A major aim of our diplomacy with Moscow should be to show the Soviet leaders that, as near neighbors of both India and China, they have more to fear than we.

In view of these truths it is clear that the most rational way to do the job would be a co-operative effort of the United States and the U.S.S.R., as the world's greatest and richest nations, to develop the resources and productive capacities of the Hungry World. It is equally clear that such an effort could be most effectively planned and co-ordinated by the UN. This would tend to spare the Hungry World the shame and hostility usually aroused in the heart of the recipient of charity, so aptly described by Confucius when he posed the question, "Why do you hate me? I never helped you."

This dream of world-wide co-operation and the unselfish sharing of wealth by those who have with those who have not found expression in the Marshall Plan. But Soviet leaders, suspicious and hostile, spurned the plan and forced their dependencies to do likewise. Subsequent suggestions of even regional or limited co-operation have been rudely rejected by Nikita Khrushchev. Behind pious pleas for peaceful co-existence, disarmament, and trade, like those so ably voiced by Comrade K. himself in the United States in September, 1959, Soviet leadership has continued indefatigably to wage the class war along the lines laid down by Marx and Lenin. Mistaken though their concepts are and obsolete as their theories have become, these attitudes have bred hostilities and suspicions on our side and made the cold war, at least for the time being, a primary reality of the modern world.

Perhaps the birth of the Common Market, the incipient industrialization of China, India, Canada, and Brazil, will reconstitute a multipower world, as Walter Rostow suggests. These new great powers may force the United States and the

U.S.S.R. to reconcile their differences and stop sowing lethal tares in each other's fields.

Indeed, I still hope to live to see realized those majestic dreams of American generosity in world-wide co-operation expressed by such men as Henry Wallace, Walter Reuther, and George Marshall. But for the moment it is clear that Soviet leaders regard co-existence as a tactical step in Communism's conquest of the world. Consequent hostilities and tensions have so nourished each other that our entire planet, including the Hungry World, has become a battlefield in the economic, military, and political struggle between two power coalitions.

THE COLD WAR FIRST

For the time being, unfortunately, the development of the Hungry World must be planned and carried out unilaterally by ourselves and our friends in the context of, and as a part of, the cold war.

I hope that political changes on both sides may soon free us all from the necessity of regarding each aspect of our national activity as an operation of political warfare. But such changes cannot be unilateral, and we must for the moment regard each policy and action in terms of its effect in the cold war.

USING OUR ASSETS

In this context we come into direct competition with the Soviet Union. Twenty-five years ago, when I first went to the Soviet Union, that country was deployed in a struggle which we then hardly knew existed, under two principal operating slogans: "Overtake and Surpass the Capitalist World" and "Socialism in One Country." During recent months I have heard stalwart Americans urge that we bend our efforts toward overtaking the Russians in order to assure the preservation of capitalism in at least one country.

Personally, I feel that the terms capitalism and socialism in this context have become so obsolete as to be virtually mean-

ingless. However, in certain key directions such as rocket research we have already been overtaken, while if that gray area
between the United States and the U.S.S.R. has not yet gone
"socialist," its "capitalist" purity has certainly been blemished.

Yet here we stand, fencing uncertainly with our opponents.
And fence we must, for while it is difficult to see at the moment how we could win the cold war, we certainly could lose it.
Let us make the best of those assets we have, while trying to
play on our opponent's shortcomings. Instead of meeting him
where he is strong, let us contrive to do battle where he is weak.

A decade ago we had nuclear bombs and they did not, and
we could perhaps have blown them up without suffering any
direct military damage. It is now too late to argue whether
such a course would have been wise or right. We did not do it,
and now, both in the bombs themselves and in their delivery,
we have lost our supremacy.

In various industrial indices such as steel production or in
the training of doctors and engineers, we have also lost our
heavy margin of superiority. And indeed, given the geographic
fact that the U.S.S.R. is twice as large as the United States
and at least as rich in resources, given their greater population and the greater intensity of their efforts, given their average
annual GNP increase rate of 8 per cent compared to our 3.5
to 4 per cent, it seems arithmetically certain, all other things
being equal, that within a generation they will have passed us
in most indices of power.

A French writer friend of mine recently overstated this
development by expressing his hope that "you Americans will
accept more gracefully than we your fall to the status of a
second-rate power."

But there is one area in which we have today and will have
for at least a decade a decided advantage: We have economic
surpluses, while the Soviet is still a deficit economy.

We have it within our power without depriving ourselves of
necessities or even of many comforts to undertake and carry

out a massive effort to develop the Hungry World, to help its nearly two billion people to feed and clothe and house themselves.

This is the obvious, logical thing for us to do. We have all the prerequisites except perhaps the imagination and the courage. For we have too much of everything. We are paying our farmers not to plant; we have nine billion dollars' worth of agricultural surpluses stored in caves; we design our clothes and cars and utilities in such a way as to fool ourselves into replacing them with new ones when they are hardly broken in. All this we have in a world more than half of whose citizens are undernourished, poorly clothed, and housed.

Can we develop the Hungry World without destroying our "American way of life"? I think we can. Further, I believe that with a proper program these economic aims can be realized without arousing the resentment and hatred of the Hungry World and also without fatally antagonizing our friends and allies.

POLITICAL POLICIES

The essence of our policy must be to win the confidence of the people of the Hungry World. Our first step should be a declaration at the highest level that the days of both political and economic colonialism are ended, that it is the aim of United States policy to see every part of the world self-governing and independent as soon as orderly transfers of power can be arranged. I believe the declaration should specifically name such symbolic trouble spots as Algeria, Kenya, Goa, Dutch New Guinea, Okinawa, Formosa, and the Belgian Congo on our side of the curtain, and Tibet, Eastern Europe's captive nations, and also such historically independent national minorities as the Balts, Georgians, and Armenians in the Soviet Union itself. In these areas we should advocate self-determination followed by integration into a free world of co-operation and prosperity.

Protests would no doubt be raised in Paris and Amsterdam, in Brussels and Lisbon. And our own Pentagon would perhaps be disturbed at the prospect of losing complete control of Okinawa.

But elementary wisdom invites us to exploit the inevitable, and wise men in every capital realize that self-determination is in the cards for the whole Hungry World and it is silly to try to stop it. A prominent Dutch banker told me recently that he saw no purpose in keeping the remote remnant of Holland's Indonesian empire that the Indonesians call West Irian. Yet some sentiment, some false pride moved the Dutch to make a major issue of this matter, with the result that about a billion dollars' worth of Dutch assets in the Indies was lost.

The French would scream at our interference with their "internal affairs" in Algeria, but they do anyhow, and such a declaration might help to settle the war in the only way it can be settled in the long run—self-determination for Algeria.

Having thus declared for the abolition of colonialism, we could then proceed to deal with several regional problems of key importance, problems for many years neglected, evaded, ignored.

CHINA POLICY

The dilemma of United States China policy is one of the most difficult.

The British recognized Peking in 1949, and it got them neither trade nor prestige. Nor did it drive any visible wedge between China and the U.S.S.R.

I traveled to the Orient recently thinking that United States China policy was uninspired and should be changed. I returned thinking that our China policy is indeed uninspired, but that any sudden radical change would be unwise.

Were the United States to extend recognition to Communist China now, the results in Southeast Asia would be immediate and negative. Both the overseas Chinese and the non-Chinese

Asians and their governments in places like Viet-Nam, Cambodia, Laos, Thailand, and the Philippines would be demoralized. The governments would have no defense against the demands of their own left to recognize Communist China, and such recognition would immediately give the Chinese new and important political strongholds in Southeast Asia. Even more serious, these governments might well conclude that United States recognition constituted the first step of a general United States withdrawal from Asia, and it might start a chain reaction of attempts of Southeast Asian nations to line themselves up on what would seem to them the winning side. Several knowledgeable American and British diplomats put it to me in almost identical words: "A sudden United States abandonment of Chiang and recognition of Peking would mean a Communist Southeast Asia within months." While this is a little extreme, I believe that it is essentially correct.

On the other hand, can we indefinitely avoid extending diplomatic recognition to the admittedly effective government of the most populous country in the world? To put it another way, how long can we pretend that the government in Taipei represents China?

It is my feeling that there are forces at work both in Formosa and on the mainland today which may within several years bring about the prerequisites of a two-China solution of our dilemma. In Taipei even high officials are today willing to recognize that the Communist government is in control of the mainland and that a Nationalist liberation is unlikely. On the mainland also there have been changes. Much of the truculence and bellicosity have left Peking's statements. Most of the Western prisoners have been released. The Chicoms have withdrawn from North Burma and, more important, from North Korea.

Under these circumstances a bid for United Nations membership might encourage the Chinese to move further in the direction of peace and co-operation with their neighbors. I believe the United States should stop trying to prevent the discussion of the China problem in the General Assembly. If the Assembly then appoints a commission to study the China question with a view to working out a way to grant Peking membership, the machinery will have been set in motion for a compromise solution and an eventual United States recognition of a perhaps more restrained Peking.

All the evidence indicates that in the long run a strong China will dominate East Asia as it has done repeatedly in the past. If Peking should try to formulate this probability in some sort of Chinese Monroe Doctrine, it would be perhaps no more presumptuous than was ours.

In view of all these considerations, it might be wise to suggest a United Nations-sponsored plebiscite on Formosa in the near future. It seems likely that the Formosans would vote for independence under UN trusteeship. This would perhaps give the aging Nationalists a place to die in dignity and give Peking a chance to evidence its good faith by accepting officially what is already for them a military reality.

ARAB-ISRAELI CONFLICT

Another thorny problem which the United States has been avoiding is the conflict between the Arabs and Israelis. I have dealt earlier with the background of this conflict. To summarize: The Israeli economy works on a $350 million-a-year subsidy in both public and private funds, almost entirely from the United States. The long-range viability of the Israeli economy is possible only given good relations with the Arab states, for whom the Israelis could perform many useful services. The Israelis' long-range security must depend on such Arab good will as the Israelis are able to inspire. The Arabs have in many ways been unreasonable and difficult, but, as the heavy majority in the Middle East, their good will will have to be sought by the Israelis.

A start could be made in the creation of this good will if Israel would:

1. Recognize moral and some financial responsibilities for the refugees; allow a token number to return to their homes in Israel, compensate the rest and help them find new homes, probably in Iraq.

2. Restrict immigration.

3. Implement at least some of the 1949 United Nations resolutions on frontiers. The internationalization of Jerusalem would be a good start.

I believe the United States should use economic and political pressures to urge the Israelis to do these things. A simple ruling of the Internal Revenue office on the tax deductibility of private funds for Israel would alone put great pressure on the Israelis. But if the Israelis refuse to compromise?

Russian arms are now coming steadily into the Middle East, to Yemen, Syria, Iraq, and Egypt. Unless the Russians can be bought off—Berlin has been suggested as a price though I would oppose any such deal—Israel's military position will soon be quite untenable and a regional war almost inevitable. Rather than allow this to happen, I believe we should consider a radical alternative policy: a United States passport and one thousand dollars to every Israeli who wants to come to the United States to live. We could absorb a million immigrants without trouble. The gambit would cost a billion dollars. But even a regional war would cost us that in the first week.

MIDDLE EAST DEVELOPMENT

An economic program for Middle East development is a necessity if the Middle East is to have peace. The immense potential of the Tigris-Euphrates Valley must be developed. The Aswan Dam must be built. Some steps have already been taken in this direction by the Iraqis and the Egyptians with oil money, United States and Soviet aid. But far more effort is needed, and it could best be made by a Middle East Development Authority, which I believe we should take the initiative in trying to organize.

It is not primarily new money that the area needs. In 1958 its oil royalties topped a billion dollars. But this income is often squandered by sheiks and kings on palaces and other foolishness or, worse, on jet fighters and tanks, which can only make trouble.

What is needed is a development program based on political co-operation—including Arab-Israeli co-operation—collective security under the United Nations aimed at regional disarmament, and economic partnership instead of exploitation. I should like to see the President appoint a committee of qualified men to draft such a program for presentation through the United Nations to the Middle Eastern states.

ALGERIAN WAR

The French cannot afford to fight the war or to win it. The French settlers were unwilling or unable in 140 years to earn the good will of the Algerians, and they will now have to pay for this failure. Either they must stay on as a minority, as the French did in Canada, or be resettled in metropolitan France. Both variants are economically quite possible.

This, I am convinced, is the solution that General de Gaulle is trying to bring about against the fanatical and unreasoned resistance of Frenchmen both at home and in Algeria. Colonialism is obsolete. Privileged white minorities in the Hungry World cannot be defended.

I should like to see the United States exert every economic and political pressure to help de Gaulle's efforts to stop this aimless war that is poisoning the atmosphere of all Africa and indeed of the whole Hungry World. The first such measure might be taken through NATO, for currently the French are using in Algeria some five NATO divisions, with American equipment furnished them as United States military aid.

RACISM

The last of the regional problems on which I believe the United States should take a firm official stand involves race relations, particularly in South Africa, where three million white Euro-peans seem bent on a spectacular suicide the world cannot afford. Largely as a result of *apartheid* and Algeria, those flat failures of Western conscience and intelligence, millions of Africans are beginning to listen to Moscow's appeals for vio-lence and revolt. For many Africans racial grievances are more important than any issue in the cold war. "What difference does it make to a blade of grass whether it is eaten by a horse or a cow?" a Ghanian diplomat told me.

Several times I heard Africans point out with great emotion that "*apartheid* is more cruel and unjust than anything the Communists do. For they attack men for their opinions or their actions as they did in Hungary and in Tibet. Men can temper their opinions and modify their actions. But we cannot change our color."

The United States should not only express disapproval of *apartheid* but use every economic and political pressure to force the authorities in these areas to adopt more reasonable attitudes and policies. Is this interference in their affairs? Per-haps. But racism today is everyone's affair. Besides, interfer-ence is sometimes salutary. History has more than justified the British for using their fleet a century and a half ago to force less principled neighbors to abandon a slave trade the con-science of the Western world could no longer countenance.

Nor should we fail to recognize the implications of this issue here in the United States. In this context the fight for civil rights and the implementation of Supreme Court decisions on segregation constitute a central truss of United States foreign policy.

It is true we have made progress in this direction, but there is no time for a leisurely settlement of these issues. The colored peoples constitute the majority of the human race, and they are fast acquiring voices and arms. We must realize our own expressed beliefs in the brotherhood of man, lest our children some dark day search frantically for a dependable Negro American willing to negotiate for the United States with an Afro-Asian superstate, outnumbering us twenty to one and armed with hydrogen bombs.

For the white man constitutes a small and shrinking racial minority in a molten world. The dark majority may very soon be tempted to thrust back at us the humiliations we taught them during our brief historical moment of supremacy.

Military Aid

The United States military aid program was born of necessity. In 1948, following a secret Communist conference in Calcutta, Communist insurrections were launched in Burma, Malaya, the Philippines. In 1950 the North Koreans attacked South Korea. From 1945 until 1954 Communist-led guerrillas fought the French and later the independent government of Viet-Nam. These attacks were in every case elaborately camouflaged in sociological, nationalistic, and ethnic slogans and programs calculated to win mass support. But essentially they were military attacks aimed at seizing power for the forces of communism. All these efforts came close to success. There were times in 1949 and 1950 when it looked very much as though the victorious Communist armies in China would go right on and engulf the whole Orient.

Today in Korea and Indochina the civil wars have been terminated by cease-fires, and South Korea and South Viet-Nam as well as Cambodia and Laos are being administered by non-Communist governments and have been made strong enough to resist any but large-scale (and unlikely) Communist military aggression. The Huk insurrection has been virtually liquidated; the Communist guerrillas in Malaya and Burma have been isolated in relatively small areas.

Southeast Asia is militarily more secure today than it has been at any time since 1949. This achievement is at least in part the result of American and British military effort and aid.

In Korea this effort was made under the flag of the United Nations. Farther south actions and aid have been made by individual governments, in some instances conducted since 1954 by SEATO.

In West Asia and Africa no Communist military actions have taken place, but fear that they might be undertaken caused the United States to extend military aid to Pakistan, Turkey, and Iran in large quantities. While the civil war went on in China, we made available some two billion dollars to Chinese Nationalist authorities and since that time have continued to give them substantial aid.

For the past decade the United States has been spending about $2.5 billion a year in direct military aid. In the Orient this aid goes to South Korea, Japan, Formosa, the Philippines, Thailand, and Pakistan. Britain extends military aid to Hong Kong and Singapore, and to Malaya, Ceylon, Jordan, and the assorted British protectorates on the Arabian peninsula. France extends military aid to Cambodia, Viet-Nam, and Laos. Actually, United States arrangements with Britain and France are such that the United States pays part of this British and French military aid.

These military efforts have had several negative consequences. In the first place, they have made it possible for the Communists to illustrate plausibly their propaganda line about the United States being a warmonger actively preparing to plunge the world into the horrors of atomic war and seeking to sell obsolete weapons and superfluous military training to unsuspecting Asians for fabulous profits.

In the second place, the presence of large numbers of United States military personnel in Asia has led to a number of embarrassing incidents which created hostility toward the United States. Three of these cases—those of Seaman George Roe in the Philippines, Technician First Class William Girard in Japan, and Sergeant Robert Reynolds in Formosa—hit the headlines and in two cases led to violence and a great deal of most unpleasant publicity about the United States, ably used by the Communists in propaganda all over the world.

In the third place, as one critic recently put it, our military aid has all too often helped our friends build armed forces incapable of fighting a modern war, on economies incapable of supporting even such establishments.

But the effectiveness of our military aid in stopping Communist aggression was conclusively demonstrated when after Stalin's death the Communists changed the emphasis of their tactics toward economic and political infiltration. The success of the new line was sobering, particularly in India, Indonesia, and parts of the Middle East. For the first time in history there is a good chance of Communist electoral victories in several large countries of the non-Communist world.

This has, in my opinion, left our aid program out of balance. If it was wise five years ago to spend annually $700 million in military aid, $300 million in economic aid in Korea, perhaps today the reverse would constitute a more appropriate ratio.

In Latin America I was disturbed by what I saw of our limited military programs. The Ecuadorians maintain a force of jet fighters. The Peruvians, Colombians, and even the Nicaraguans have expensive military equipment obtained mostly from the United States. In the majority of Latin American countries United States military and air missions help the local governments to train their armed forces and construct military installations, mostly as a part of "hemisphere defense."

It is fairly obvious that in case of a major war the Latin American countries could at best give but token aid in the defense of the hemisphere—in the extremely unlikely event that the Russians tried to invade it. It is equally obvious that the armed forces of each Latin American country constitute a potential threat to its neighbors, who therefore feel forced to increase their own military strength. The question asks itself: Might not this be a good time and place to promote regional disarmament? Let the United Nations and the United States guarantee Latin American frontiers and security, and the Latin American republics could save the roughly 4 per cent of their combined gross national product currently going for military purposes. If invested in well-chosen capital formation, this sum would make a substantial contribution to increased productivity, higher living standards, and greater political stability.

When I posed this question to members of various American military missions, I was answered in most cases with a shrug. But one United States ambassador gave me an answer of classic lucidity: "These little countries have got to have armed forces; otherwise, they'd be invading each other all the time."

The real reason for the armies, of course, is to keep current governments in power. And the main purpose of the military missions is to secure and maintain influence in the armed forces which are so necessary to their governments. These circumstances, unfortunately, render it unlikely that any regional disarmament in Latin America will soon become a practical possibility.

Economic Aid

Since the end of World War II the United States has extended economic aid to about sixty countries in the world, totaling about fifty billion dollars. Of this only a small part has gone to the Hungry World. Most of it has gone to Britain, Germany, and France. Currently, the administration is trying to increase the proportion of direct aid going to Asia and Africa. Asia is now getting about one billion dollars a year from the United States in direct economic aid. Africa gets about $100 million. In Latin America only small sums have gone in economic aid, almost entirely to Bolivia. The biggest recipients of economic aid have been Korea, Viet-Nam, Turkey, Formosa, India, and Pakistan. All these but India are allies of the United States and hosts of our bases.

The purpose of United States aid is to prevent the disease

and unrest on which communism thrives and to help create
viable nations, capable of supporting and defending themselves
against direct or indirect aggression. United States aid is not
aimed at gratitude. Nor should it be. The powerful are sometimes respected, often feared, but almost never loved. This the
British learned two centuries ago. Today many adolescent Americans want desperately to be loved and feel angry and hurt
when fleeced by the concierge in Paris, told to "go home" by
crowds in Baghdad, or stoned in La Paz.

Our economic aid has been directed to those sectors of the
recipients' economy that seemed to the competent International
Cooperation Administration official most important. Often the
recipients' leaders resent this "interference" in their internal
affairs. Sometimes, angered, they accuse the United States of
using aid as a mechanism for getting rid of surpluses and obso-
lescent equipment, rather than for helping others solve their
problems. The Communists add fuel to these fires of resentment.

I have strong opinions as to the use of economic aid. To
build simultaneously four steel mills in India, one of whose
primary problems is unemployment, was, I think, foolish indeed.
For no enterprises, except possibly chemical plants, produce
fewer new jobs per unit of capital invested than steel mills. The
Indians would have been well advised to spend part of the half-
billion-dollar steel mill bill on modernizing agriculture and
local transport and perhaps on light industry, where more jobs
would have been created and where the return on the investment
would have been quicker.

On the other hand, to put all one's aid into consumer goods
or light industry would be foolish, too, for as then President
"Pepe" Figueras of Costa Rica told me, "A nation grows not
on what it produces, but on what it saves."

With reference to these latter arguments as to the form and
use of United States aid, I favor in principle long-term loans
at low interest rather than gifts, channeled into efforts determined in the last instance by the recipient. But advice and

counsel should be generously offered to help the recipient decide wisely.

In this respect, as in many others, I believe it is useful to have our aid channeled when possible through the organs of the United Nations or through a world economic development fund. For advice offered by such a body would tend, like the aid itself, to be more acceptable to the recipient.

In general, I believe our economic aid has in the past been well worth while, though I regret the fact that so much went for military hardware, so little proportionately to the Hungry World.

In the future I would like to see the United States help organize a vast program of economic aid administered by a world development fund in co-operation with representatives of the recipient nations and aimed at accomplishing these objectives in this order:

1. Prevent catastrophes of hunger and disease. Assure minimal diet and emergency medical aid.

2. Assure a capital formation rate of at least 15 per cent.

3. Channel developmental funds into the most appropriate sector of the economy as determined by geography, economic development, and the wishes of the recipient.

4. Provide for the expenditure of at least 5 per cent of the GNP on education.

5. Channel aid through local private enterprise where this is possible in order to encourage the development of a local middle class.

Such a program might be calculated at 1 per cent of the GNP of the "have" nations, which might include as a beginning the United States, Canada, Great Britain, and the Common Market, and thus dispose some seven billion dollars a year.

In this context the current treatment by the United States of our agricultural surpluses as embarrassing liabilities and of our productivity as a curse to be bought off by indulgences to our farmers is both destructive and shocking. Our explosive agricultural productivity complements the race's explosive reproductivity, and should, according to any natural law, be used to feed the hungry mouths in areas which have not yet reaped the bounty of the soil augmented by better techniques and seeds and fertilizers. Our stocks of foods and fibers already produced, plus those we would have if we used instead of contraceiving our productivity, would go far toward starting such a fund.

Foundations and Charities

Between governmental aid and private capital investment lies the field of activity of the foundations and dozens of religious and secular charities. I have mentioned earlier the fine work of the Ford Foundation in India, the Asia Foundation in the Orient, the Schweitzer Foundation in Africa, Operation Brotherhood. I could also have expressed my admiration for the work I saw being done by CARE, Meals for Millions, and dozens of religious missions and schools all over the Hungry World. All have done well, and their work should be continued and expanded.

Private Investment

There is no argument on the desirability of increasing capital investments in underdeveloped areas. The need is apparent. But here a dilemma arises. American investors are loath to lend money in underdeveloped nations at "normal" rates of interest because the return would not justify the risks. The governments of the new nations, on the other hand, are under heavy political pressure not to allow "excessive profits" or "economic colonialism" and not to "sell their country's wealth to foreign imperialist concessionaires."

Conscious of the importance of this issue, Time Inc. organized an inter-American investment conference in New Orleans in 1955, and Stanford University and Time Inc. co-sponsored the

International Industrial Development Conference in San Francisco in October 1957 to try to bring together American investors and overseas businessmen to discuss investment possibilities and methods of overcoming difficulties.

At the San Francisco Conference both in brilliant speeches and in private talks, a number of concrete proposals were discussed. Among these the following seemed oustanding:

1. Things the United States Government might do:

a. Income taxes on the profits on investments in underdeveloped areas might be deferred until the profits are distributed as dividends to the investors.

b. Income tax credits similar to those for which Western Hemisphere corporations are already eligible might be extended to investors in underdeveloped areas everywhere.

c. The United States might finally lower or abolish tariffs, thus making it easier for foreign debtors to service or repay their obligations to United States creditors.

d. The United States Department of Justice might relax on Sherman Act prosecution sufficiently to allow United States companies operating abroad enough collusion to defend their interests against Communist monopolies.

2. Things the businessmen of all countries might do:

a. An international credit fund might be formed to facilitate long-term credit so that underdeveloped countries could make necessary purchases.

b. A Magna Charta for investments might be formulated, spelling out the rights and responsibilities of investors. Nations whose governments failed to sign the Magna Charta could expect trouble in getting investments. Signatories would get the co-operation of an association of investors formed under the Magna Charta.

Underlying these specifics are three general issues, which I believe deserve attention. The first is the question of the form of investments in underdeveloped areas.

PARTNERSHIPS

It has long been obvious that concessions are outmoded. The new nations of the Hungry World do not want to sell their resources; they want to become partners in their development.

This is already being done by some oil companies who, in effect, are in business partnerships with governments like that of Venezuela and with private corporations in countries like Japan.

To spell out one specific case, the Caltex Corporation and Caltex Oil Products are two prime companies of the Caltex Group, incorporated in the United States and based in New York. The Caltex Corporation holds 50 per cent of the stock in the Nippon Petroleum Refining Company, and Caltex Oil Products holds 50 per cent in the Koa Oil Company. The other 50 per cent in both cases is owned by Japanese investors. The Nippon Petroleum Refining Company owns three refineries at Yokohama, Kudamatsu, and Muroran (Hokkaido). The Koa Oil Company owns a refinery at Marifu (southern Honshu). The Nippon Oil Company, besides owning 50 per cent of the stock of the Nippon Petroleum Refining Company, also markets the entire finished product offtake from NPRC's three refineries and KOA's one refinery, under an offtake agreement. Caltex Japan acts as co-ordinator of all the Caltex interests in Japan. Tokyo Tanker Company owns several large tankers for hauling the crude oil from Arabia and Sumatra to Japan. Its stock is owned 50-50 by NPRC and KOA, and thus Caltex has an effective 50 per cent interest through its holdings in these companies.

Another kind of partnership has been established by the Coca-Cola Company in many parts of the world. The company—and many of its competitors do the same thing—goes to a foreign country, finds an able man with initiative and perhaps a little capital, and helps him set up a bottling business. The Coca-Cola Company gets its profit by selling concentrate to the bottler, with whom it thereby creates a partnership relation. Of course, Coca-Cola is not the most important thing in the world for most retarded countries, but the fact that the operation has been successful indicates the soundness of the corporate principle used.

The advantages of these partnership arrangements in any of their forms are obvious. The United States partner finds an outlet for both his capital and management enterprise and also gains access to valuable raw materials whose domestic supplies may be limited. The underdeveloped country gets capital, employment for its people, and is itself a partner in its own development. Most important of all, the partnership is the investor's best guarantee against expropriation.

Still experimental but most promising is the triple partnership. This presents the general advantage of any partnership plus added attractions for the semi-developed countries. The general lines of the triple partnership were spelled out by Japanese Prime Minister Kishi: the use of American capital and Japanese technology for the development of the resources and the markets of underdeveloped countries.

The triple partnership principle has been suggested also by the Japanese on the governmental level and has been implemented in some arrangements between the ICA, the Japanese, and Viet-Nam. But serious difficulties must be overcome: (a) United States Congress' reluctance to appropriate money for vicarious aid; and (b) Japan's unpopularity among the Asians she so recently tried to force by fire and sword into Japan's wartime Greater East Asian Co-Prosperity Sphere.

I was delighted recently to hear an American Oil Company executive make the following remark: "Confiscatory action by the Arab states of our concessions is just a matter of time—months rather than years. Why not anticipate this by *giving* our concessions to the people of these states and concluding partnership-management agreements with them for operations and marketing?" No details were discussed, but in my opinion such courageous thinking is essential if the oil companies are to survive in the Middle East.

On the other side, I was shocked and saddened recently at a New York lunch with some executives of one of our largest banks to learn that they were establishing branches rather than partnerships in Africa. "Partnerships cannot be formed. It is against the banking laws and against our policy, too." It is high time both were changed.

INVESTMENTS IN LATIN AMERICA

United States private investments in Latin America have been far larger than in Asia or Africa, averaging about $500 million a year. But this represents barely 3 per cent of the total annual private investment of Latin America. Furthermore, the greater part of United States capital invested in Latin America represents the reinvested profits from old investments. In 1958 total profits on United States investments in Latin America were greater than total investments, i.e., more wealth went from Latin America to the United States than passed in the other direction.

At New Orleans several Latin American statesmen expressed their resentment of this "exploitation." This resentment is based at least in part on a failure to evaluate diverse forms of investment. These include the 500 fellowships for Latin American students to study abroad contributed each year by United States private companies. This is an investment in hard currency which the Latin Americans themselves tend not to regard as such. Currently, 727 fellowships are also offered annually by the technical co-operation program of the UN and 200 by the Organization of American States. Many foreign companies send to their associate or subsidiary companies in Latin America new equipment, technical processes, patents and designs, none of which appears on the books in financial terms. Since World War II, the Export-Import Bank, an agency of the United States Government, loaned $2.2 billion of United States taxpayers' money in Latin America. The International Bank for Reconstruction and Development invested $280,400,000 in Latin America. Latin American critics frequently fail to take these facts into consideration.

But there is no doubt that the Latin Americans have a point. For in 1958, a good year, the per capita income in Latin America failed to increase, the increase in gross product being just about matched by the area's fabulous nearly 3-per-cent population increase. This is a most unhealthy situation and one bound to cause political complications.

What should be done? Increase investments, preferably in partnerships, in Latin America. Latin America needs more capital. The United Nations Economic Commission for Latin America is urging a concerted effort to raise foreign investments in Latin America to a minimum of one billion dollars a year. Fidel Castro's plea in May 1959 for thirty billion "gringo" dollars over the next ten years for Latin American development may have been crudely formulated, but its reception indicated the reality of the need.

ALLOCATION

A third major issue in the field of investment is: What should we invest in?

So far United States investors have tended to regard the Hungry World essentially as a source of raw materials and primary crops—copper, gold, oil, phosphates, cocoa, coffee. This is the way Europe regarded the United States until the middle of the nineteenth century. When the Europeans changed the emphasis of their investments and began building factories and mills, everyone benefited.

Let us consider the Hungry World as more than a billion human beings currently living close to subsistence, who would like to become both producers and consumers. To help them make this leap ahead is to create new markets for commodities and for processes and techniques. Interesting and challenging job opportunities for scores of thousands of Western technicians will at the same time be created. This in turn will form the basis for the most important prerequisite for a peaceful and prosperous world partnership.

The Future

During my journeys through the Hungry World, I heard many intelligent voices raised in criticism of the United States for not investing more private and public funds in the world's retarded nations. In the twenty-four years from 1929 until 1953 United States gross national product increased more than four times, they pointed out, while direct investments abroad merely doubled. Many continued with a poignant argument: "When America was young, when you were building your factories and railroads, billions of dollars came into the United States from European investors. Now you are failing to pass along the favor to us."

But these reproaches raise a counter-question. What is the future of our relations to the Hungry World? Must we look forward to a permanent government giveaway program to keep what many Americans view as indolent natives from rebelling against their inefficient and corrupt governments, while private capital is poured into huge developmental projects ripening for nationalization? And if successful, are not our efforts simply creating competitors for our own industries?

In both cases the answer, I think, is no. As living standards rise and literacy increases, as the middle class grows and learns, as the underdeveloped countries reach what Professor Rostow calls the economic take-off point, after which they become airborn, their economic development becomes self-sustaining. They become large-scale consumers and investors.

Look at the Japanese. They no longer require aid and are

already in a position through the Kishi Plan to co-operate with the United States in extending aid to their neighbors. And if they are competitors for a few American manufacturers, they are a market for many more.

More instructive, let me suggest the analogy of British aid and investments sent to the United States in the nineteenth century. The aid was delivered under the protection of the British fleet, which sheltered United States interests and business abroad until World War I. Investment figures are difficult to obtain, but it seems likely that the British invested fifty billion dollars or so in the United States before 1913. Not only did it pay dividends, but it created a valuable market for British goods in the United States and furnished Britain with sources of raw materials which it badly needed as its own became exhausted. Of course, some of the young United States industries competed with their English cousins, but the competition was probably salutary for both and led to new desires and new markets in both countries.

Surely this is a pattern for a healthy, mutually beneficial relationship between an underdeveloped dependent nation and a highly industrialized parent-partner.

I should like to see us spend 10 per cent of our GNP, as Britain did in 1900, on aid and investments overseas, instead of the less than 1 per cent we spent last year. I should like to see it channeled more and more into manufacturing and processing as the economics of the world's new nations develop. I agree most heartily with Eugene Black's recent pleas for "quality" as well as quantity in our investments.

Most important, these investments should be expressed in partnerships. For the very word embodies the concept of brotherhood so deeply rooted in the Judeo-Christian ethic we profess; it embodies the concept of economic co-operation and the idea of racial harmony, both so necessary in dealing with the Hungry World.

CULTURAL AND EDUCATIONAL ACTIVITY

In the area of culture and education much has been done; more remains to do. There is, in my opinion, no better investment in the future than scholarships and exchanges.

In this, as in other areas, the USIA has done well on a shamefully small budget.

With the limited resources made available by Congress, the USIA has been hammering away over radio, through the press, and other media at the central fact that Communist colonialism today is far more exploitative than any Western imperialism has been for fifty years. Moscow and Peking are today the principal threats to national independence in the Hungry World.

Communism is trying in Asia to use nationalism and the vague, outmoded Asian concept of socialism to seize and hold power. In using this power to deprive Asians of their national independence and their control over their own economies and resources, the men of Moscow are turning Lenin on his head and demonstrating that imperialism is the final stage of moribund communism.

The USIA assures the nations of the Hungry World that we want them to have the fullest national independence and whatever measure of public control over their economies they themselves freely decide is desirable and are willing, nay anxious, to help them realize both aims.

The adoption by the United States Government of those principles and objectives stated at the beginning of this chapter would render more effective the work of the USIA.

TRADE UNIONS

Trade unions are particularly important in the Hungry World because they appeal to and help the newly born working class, the principal target of Communist efforts.

Unions are new in Africa, but already they have had an immense effect. The International Confederation of Free Trade

Unions (ICFTU) alone has twenty-one affiliates in eighteen African territories and countries, with a total membership of well over one million. Other unaffiliated unions and a few associated with the World Federation of Trade Unions in Prague bring the total up close to 1.5 million members, which is remarkable in consideration of the fact that in the continent's principal industrial power, the Union of South Africa, native unions have been outlawed; while at the other end of the continent, in Egypt, the unions are not considered free but, on the contrary, government organizations.

The ICFTU maintains regional offices in Nairobi and Accra and currently is working toward the formation of new trade unions in the Union of South Africa, Ethiopia, and the Portuguese territories, where such organizations are at present banned.

The African trade-union movement has produced some of the most vigorous and talented nationalist leaders; and the chances seem good that it will continue to do so, particularly in view of the absence in most of Africa of a middle-class intellectual elite. I talked with a number of African labor leaders about the necessity of keeping labor productivity increases above their wage demands and found general agreement on this issue. But the unions are most active in fighting for equal pay for equal work for African labor and also take a strong stand on such political issues as the support of the Algerian nationalists in their struggle for independence.

In India, Ceylon, and Indonesia unions are strong. In Turkey, Egypt, and most of the Middle East unions are forbidden or are organs of the government.

The trade-union movement is fairly vigorous in Latin America. In many cases the unions are government-controlled and are anti-Communist, as in Venezuela and the Argentine. In other cases, they are independent and anti-Communist under the general aegis of ORIT (Organizacion Regional Inter-Americana de Trabajadores), which has about twenty-five million members, of whom fifteen million are in the AFL-CIO and the Canadian trade unions. Half of the Latin American members are in three countries: 2,500,000 in Brazil, 1,250,000 in Mexico, and 1,200,000 in Cuba. The rest are scattered throughout the other Latin American states. ORIT does not recognize the Mexican Electrical Workers Union, which is Communist dominated, nor the Argentine and Venezuelan government unions.

Throughout the Hungry World trade unions constitute one of the most important barriers to Communist infiltration. If dealt with fairly and properly, they can also play a major role in raising labor productivity and in education. The prejudiced views of administrators unable to comprehend the trade union movement can only inhibit economic progress and introduce additional divisive elements into the political ferment of the Hungry World.

PERSONNEL

The recently published book, *The Ugly American*, has focused attention on the mischief wrought in many parts of the world by misled or malicious American servicemen and public servants.

And such men and women there certainly are. Nor could it be otherwise, when we have some 750 military bases overseas, staffed by nearly half a million servicemen plus more than a million American tourists, businessmen, and students going abroad every year.

In my travels I met a number of Americans who reflected little credit on their country, largely through the thoughtless ostentation of their way of spending money. The authors of *The Ugly American*, I believe, did a service in bringing this matter to public attention, and it may make many Americans more conscious of their responsibilities while abroad.

But I believe that for every "ugly American" in our many missions abroad, there are a dozen honest and dedicated servants of the United States, filling well their frequently difficult missions.

That even the best Americans abroad are frequently maligned is not surprising.

As at least temporary heirs to a large measure of world leadership, we are the target of criticism, envy, and hostility, irrespective of our performance.

But some of our unpopularity is earned and avoidable. Some selectivity in the choice of American officials to serve in sensitive posts abroad could save much friction. And I personally would go further and impose on American officials, business and professional men bound for foreign posts some succinct briefing and some screening before they leave our shores. The political West Point suggested by Representatives Herlong and Judd could make possible major improvements in this direction.

If Democracy Is not Enough, What Is?

We arrive at our final central question. If multi-party parliamentary democracy will not work in the Hungry World during its turbulent development through self-government and independence, education, and capital formation, what will work? How are the world's eager new nations to govern themselves?

I believe that such leaders as Viet-Nam's President Diem, Kenya's Tom Mboya, Tanganyika's Julius Nyerere, and Tunisia's Habib Bourguiba are on the right track. A limited and temporary authoritarianism is necessary. To repeat and paraphrase the words of one African nationalist leader: "For some time we will have to be careful whom we let the people vote for. Our people must be guided by a disciplined elite group who know what the country needs and take effective steps to achieve it."

Although individuals like Kemal Ataturk have done well indeed in such positions, men are mortal. I personally am driven to conclude that the instrument best fitted to do this job is a political party, working in every private and public institution in the country, leading, cajoling, warning, inspiring. It is such parties that Julius Nyerere and Tom Mboya are currently trying

to organize in their countries, and we would be blind not to
see that in their structure and functions these parties will probably be far more similar to the Communist parties in the curtain
countries than to the loose-knit political parties of the United
States, Britain, or France.

How do we guard against the power-lusting leader who over-
stays his mandate as countless dictators in the Hungry World
have done? How do we prevent the elite political party from
becoming a Communist party, dedicated to perpetual dictatorship and participation in world conquest?

The answer lies, I think, in an effective system of checks and
controls, a federation of political parties dedicated to guiding
their countries through the precipitous rapids of development.
We must then encourage such federation to exercise guidance
and restraint on the member parties.

Only healthy, prosperous, self-governing nations in the Hungry World can be capable of resisting direct or indirect aggression. It will take years for these nations to acquire the assets and
education needed to institute democracy. While our policies
must point in this direction, the more immediate task is to aid
and protect these new nations during their processes of capital
formation and education.

It is *for* such nations rather than *against* the U.S.S.R. or China
or communism that the United States must bend its efforts.

To achieve this objective, democracy is not enough.

The continuation and expansion of our aid programs, administered by well-chosen and able men and women and ably
publicized and merchandised by a reinforced USIA also falls
short of what is needed.

The formulation of clear policies, identifying ourselves with
the aspirations of the peoples of the Hungry World for freedom
and independence in a majestic program under the United
Nations is also something less than is needed.

The expansion of our investment programs in a huge effort
to share the bounty of our economy, to develop in partnership

with our less affluent fellow men their resources and energies, while most necessary, is still not enough to achieve our aims.

To accept benevolent, temporarily authoritarian governments, led by political associations, guided and advised by the best men we can find in our country and led by the ablest and most dedicated men in each underdeveloped land is still not enough.

Something else is needed.

Communist parties are effective not merely because they are disciplined and unscrupulous but because they have an ideology. The Communists have a closed system of beliefs. They have answers to all questions. One can dispute their premises, attack their logic, deny their conclusions. But they have positive positions, a positive philosophy.

Our positions are pragmatic and relative. Nor is this surprising, for our ideology is associated with the pragmatism and relativism of John Dewey and Oliver Wendell Holmes. And pragmatism is the negation of a positive ideology.

As long as our orientation is tied to Dewey and Holmes, it will be difficult for us to formulate or implement a positive foreign policy or to help create a community of viable, vigorous, and self-sufficient nations able to defend themselves against Communist aggression and even subvert the Communists themselves with more virile convictions.

Why then do we not formulate a new and virile ideology to knit together the organizations we could launch and nourish?

The answer is simple. We are overfed, overindulged egocentrics. We are pampered, petulant, and selfish individualists, suspended in a state Reinhold Niebuhr calls "sophisticated vulgarity." We are unwilling to implement the ritual we mouth on Sundays and share with our neighbors. We have contrived a series of deals with pseudo-truth which has left us bloated with food and drink but ideologically naked.

For too many of us the brotherhood of man has degenerated into a glorification of the rugged individual and his ability to acquire and keep more material goods than the neighbor he does not love. Our opponents, on the contrary, subordinate the interests of the individual to the group—to society. Although this concept is shamelessly and consistently violated by the Soviet leaders in their dealings with each other, with their people, and with other nations, it still inspires men both in their country and abroad to effort and sacrifice so effectively used by Communist parties in realizing their aims.

We have in our recent heritage every prerequisite for positive thought. Martin Luther may have argued vehemently with Rome as to what the truth was, but neither questioned its existence. Emanuel Kant's categorical imperative insisted that man is truly free only when he does what he *should*.

I am no theologian, but I think I am journalist enough to perceive that if we do not rediscover some measure of truth, we may shortly lose far more than the Hungry World.